Confessions of a Pretty Lady

Confessions of a Pretty Lady

Sandra Bernhard

1817

HARPER & ROW, PUBLISHERS, New York

Cambridge, Philadelphia, San Francisco

London, Mexico City, São Paulo, Singapore, Sydney

Portions of this work previously appeared in *Interview* and *Vanity Fair*.

In some instances names have been changed and characters have been made up. These are indicated by an asterisk following the names.

FIRST EDITION

Copy editor: Marjorie Horvitz
Designer: Erich Hobbing

Library of Congress Cataloging-in-Publication Data
Bernard, Sandra.
  Confessions of a pretty lady.

  1. Bernhard, Sandra. 2. Actors—United States—Biography. 3. Comedians
—United States—Biography. I. Title.
PN2287.B4375A3 1988   792'.028'0924 [B]   87-46116
ISBN 0-06-015929-4

88 89 90 91 92 DT/HC 10 9 8 7 6 5 4 3 2 1

Acknowledgments

Special thanks to
my family, Craig Nelson, John Boskovich
and all my maids . . .

"When I was just a little girl, I asked my mother,
'What would I be? Would I be pretty? Would I be rich?'
Here's what she said to me . . ."

—Doris Day

Someone calls from the midst of their Christmas crisis, somewhere from the cold flat badlands of the American Midwest, where all dreams are born and radiate east and west.

I am alone and hating these stupid traditions that make people drink too much and drive loaded weapons up and down Ventura Freeway. But there is no escaping it; it's an imposition that I can't ignore. I throw around some red ribbons and bows and join in the mall frenzy, buying those special gifts.

I come into my clean apartment, where everything is always in place, where organization rules. I am safe here, among my things: a black couch with a foldaway bed; three bright-blue chairs with metal arms, which you put together yourself; a tall, thin brass lamp with a halogen bulb that should burn for twenty-five years as long as no one ever touches it; a glass-top table with four black chairs that match the blue ones, and a view of the valley.

I broil whitefish in my spacious kitchen and wash dishes in Palmolive liquid. There are two bathrooms—one with a shower stall and one with a bathtub/shower combination. Hanging on the wall are two pictures I stole from the California Hotel in Santa Barbara. My office has two monolithic filing cabinets containing relics of bad business relationships. My bedroom changes with the seasons: in winter there's a green flannel comforter with assorted red flannel sheets; in summer we move into a Greek Islands feel, with a stucco-colored comforter, ocean-blue sheets and striped pillowcases.

For my few possessions I am thankful; slowly I gather the accoutrements that force me into adulthood.

Before I was born, for a few Christmases my mom would have a tree. She grew up around a lot of Gentile people, and all her best girlfriends were Christian. I remember going over to visit them on the outskirts of Flint, in small, cozy houses with dinette sets, childless, with hairdos they gave themselves (Toni home perms and such), husbands with slight pompadours and graying temples, chain-smoking Kents.

My mom would talk about college days, which were brief because the war broke out and my grandfather needed her to come home and work in the junkyard. She had saved up a thousand dollars and was headed down to South America to study art and stay with a girl she had met from there, but then she met my dad, who was doing his internship at a small hospital in Jackson. He was the first man she ever really went out with, and everyone thought for sure she was destined to be an old maid, so my grandmother really lassoed my father—"so skinny he was, all bones; I made dinner for him every night"—and he grew to love my mom although she wasn't the kind of woman he was used to. He liked them wild and more bitchy and sophisticated, which she was the antithesis of—so shy and withdrawn.

All the bridesmaids wore different dresses at the wedding. My dad in his wire-rimmed glasses looked oh, so confident; my mom quiet and in another world.

He moved them out to Oregon after a year or so in a little town called Leslie, Mich., where, late at night, they would eat raw-onion-and-butter sandwiches and have fun.

On the night I was conceived, my father told my mother he needed her.

Through the years, she's told me that many times. I think of my dad vulnerable, lying on his back with deep feelings stirring in his heart, a heart he never imagined, with feelings he never admitted to anyone.

To this fragile woman, who barely believed in herself, he's telling her things she never expected to hear. At this moment, as I'm coming into my essential first seconds, they both feel so close and pure. Many things will happen as I grow, but it was in that instant when I was conceived that their world was perfect.

I walked down the driveway with my dad. All along the street there were wire garbage cans with burning fall leaves. Sparks flew into the air, and the driveway seemed to go on for miles. "Come on, you little sputnik." I held my dad's hand to go light our garbage and set our leaves on fire.

We talked quietly as he threw matches. We talked about the night sky and rockets—little stories we made up on the spot. He wore Kreml in his hair (it was like an oil-and-vinegar dressing to slick back your hair but also to stimulate its growth). He'd shake up the bottle and sprinkle it through his hair and massage it into his scalp. Running his comb under the hottest water the sink would make, he'd put a part along his right side.

He blew his nose in the sink and washed it all down and wiped up the water on the counter with his hand towel.

I'd sit with him while he ate the breakfast he made for himself—matzoh and instant coffee, toast with blueberry jam.

We'd talk in the morning before he left for rounds at the hospital.

My father never liked Tinkerbell. We got her on a trade-in on an English bulldog named Brigitte (after Bardot), which my brother Dan had for his bar mitzvah. Brigitte had congenital hip dysplasia and couldn't control her bowels, so we had to return her. I never saw my brother so dejected. Instead of giving us another bulldog, they gave us Tink, a miniature Boston terrier with a hump on her back. Dan couldn't stand the sight of her; it was a constant reminder of his betrayal. My father gave her speed one time, and she got crazy and chased herself around in circles until she collapsed on the patio.

My mom loved her, though, and Tink would sit next to her with those little bug eyes, shivering whenever my father walked in. I would sing "Around the World in Eighty Days," and she'd jump up on me as if we were both in some corny musical.

My father blamed it on his "gypsy, *Ziguener* blood": He kept moving the family around every couple of years. He took my mother and my oldest brother, who was still a baby, from Michigan out to Oswego, Oregon. Along mountain roads, the tires (made out of inferior material, right after the war) developed big balloons, which could have exploded and sent them plunging over a deserted cliff. My brother Dave was born out in Oregon. My father tired of the rain and headed back to Flint.

I spilled an entire can of redwood stain over my little tennis shoes and socks. My dad wiped them off with paint thinner and banished me to my room, where I watched him in the backyard from my window, staining the fence with my brothers. Muffin, the Kaufmans' dog, ate bread with old cooked vegetables and sour milk. Muffin threw up later on our fence. Ben Kaufman accused my dad of poisoning Muff because of the rats the fence attracted. "Don't you talk that way to me, Ben Kaufman!" "Don't you talk that way to me, Jerry Bernhard!"

My father had a Benzedrine menthol inhaler, a half-empty roll of peppermint Life Savers, jujubes, a penlight, assorted change, and plastic collar stays placed neatly in an oak desktop arranger in the exact same spot for eighteen years.

In the glove compartment of his many Pontiacs and Buicks, he kept a small-size Ozium room spray, to kill the smell of little kids and Kent cigarettes. With one hand on the wheel, he would read road maps and discipline the boys at the same time. My mother would yell, "Jerry, gee whiz, watch out for that car!" He would swerve. "For Christ's sake, I was nowhere near the goddamn thing! Shit, don't do that to me, please."

On Sundays we'd drive to one of the two inns in Frankenmuth, Mich. One, a Swiss-chalet affair, was called the Bavarian Inn, and the other, down the road, was a southern mansion called Zender's. They served family-size portions of fried chicken and mashed potatoes. The owner, an old Greek, would pass out plastic wallets to the kids. We'd usually meet the Kaufmans—Joe and Naomi and their brood of six. The Bavarian Inn was preferred. Joe and my dad would talk loudly about medicine and about doctors having affairs with their nurses.

My father studied hypnosis from records he sent away for, the Dave Ellman Technique. On Sunday afternoons, he would sit in the living room with his feet propped up and listen to these records on his brand-new Fisher stereo system (if anybody as much as dared to touch it, they'd be dead meat). "Have the subject count backward from one hundred, ninety-nine, ninety-eight, ninety-seven and so on until he seems to be in a total state of relaxation. Tell him his eyelids are growing heavy. Lift up his arm and drop it; suggest it is as limp as a wet dishcloth." I would stand just outside the living room, looking in, waiting patiently for the record to end so I could hang out with Dad.

Over the years, whenever anything was wrong I'd ask my dad for some hypnosis, and all my deepest fears and neuroses seemed to vanish. A sense of calm would come over me.

In fourth grade, I had a terrible outbreak of hives all over my body. I felt so bad, my dad had to come to school to pick me up. When we got home, my mom made us cucumber-and-nut sandwiches. My dad gave me hypnosis, and before my very eyes, the hives went down. I felt grateful, and at the same time guilty.

My mother used to tell us this story about how my father cured one of his patients of his homosexuality; she was very proud of it. She would never tell us who it was, though we would beg her for hours, guessing and laughing hysterically about who it might be. Now, years later, she still won't tell. I used to wonder what exactly my dad did to get this guy "back on the right track." I wondered if the patient had just thought about being homosexual or actually gone out and done it.

Sometime later, a butcher in Flint, who I never

really knew, killed himself by cutting off his head with an electric meat saw.

"When I was just a little girl, I asked my mother what will I be: Will I be pretty, will I be sweet . . ."

Grammy Allen gave me the Doris Day 45 and I wore it out on the hi-fi in the basement, where we would watch sci fi movies like *The Colossal Man* on Friday nights, sitting on a shiny green couch.

Grammy Allen had a mustard-seed ring and was a member of the Eastern Star. She was born in Ireland. "God damn the Catholics," she would say. She always looked sixty-five and took care of us whenever my parents were out of town. I was five when they went to Europe, abandoning me. I didn't eat for a month. I would chew my food and spit it into a napkin, then excuse myself and go to the bathroom to flush it down the toilet. Grammy would come up behind me to look at what was in there, but I flushed it before she could see.

At her house, a shillelagh leaned against a vinyl hassock next to an overstuffed nubby brown couch. The couch had small lace doilies on its inlaid wood arms and a big one covering the curve on the top, and it always felt hot to the touch. Against one wall was an armoire, packed with Limoges china and crystal goblets and beautiful linens, neatly folded. There were tiny bulbs with mustard seeds suspended in them; I would finger them and ask her what they meant every time I saw her.

In her kitchen she made "little girls' tea" in miniature china cups with tiny spoons. I sipped it on afternoons when my mom would drop me off along with the ironing. Grammy made shortbread, marshmallow balls with crushed chocolate wafers, coconut custard and lemon meringue tarts. I'd play in the bedroom with a black baby doll she kept for her granddaughters' visits.

She would pick on my brother David, blame him for everything. After his bar mitzvah, she would call him a "big-shot barmitzen," because according to Grammy, David forced her granddaughter Janet to eat a Dairy Queen, after which she threw up. Grammy yelled at David, "You're nothing but a Dairy Sucker, is what you are." But I know he let Janet throw it out onto the railroad tracks, and later I overheard Grammy on the phone with her Eastern Star crony Kate Monroe, telling her that Janet had swallowed some grape seeds and that's probably what made her sick.

Her grandson Dale was allergic to feathers, so David put some into his pillow case. When predictably he woke up wheezing, it was "the straw that broke the camel's back." Everyone was always busting David for something.

My brother Dan would sit in the dark basement for hours, smoking a pack of Marlboros and burning holes in the cellophane wrapper. He wore tweed jackets and listened to Bob Dylan, brooding, spending a lot of time with his thoughts.

It scared everyone. My father thought he was crazy and spoiled and filled with screwed-up ideas about Unitarianism, pot and sex. Dan was a good writer, but that didn't fare too well around the house. "Get those thoughts out of your head!" was the motto, but I don't think that interested him as he pondered life in 1963.

I remember the night he left home upon receiving my father's ultimatum that he either live by Dad's rules or make it on his own. I was upstairs in bed when he made the decision to leave, in his sandals with socks and his wire-rim glasses, clutching a Bible, Jack Kerouac's *On the Road* and a Honey Bear for instant energy. My heart really went out to him: I always felt pride that he'd had the guts to get out. He hitched a ride to Kansas City, where he began to work for my grandmother's second husband in his auto-parts business. He traveled around for a long time before I saw him again.

My Mom broke down the day my brother spilled a bucket of water on the wood floor of his bedroom. She ran out and threw herself on the bed. "That floor will never be the same —it's ruined!" "Don't worry, Mommy." I held her and stroked her cheek. "I'll take care of it." And I did, organizing everyone, giving directions, covering my mother with the afghan she had knitted. Afterward, what is a five-year-old girl to do but collapse in a heap, take a hot bath, sneak into her father's stash of Barton's Almond Kisses in the original tins, on which a Parisian lady walked a French poodle that extended all the way around the circumference.

Concord Street, if you walked far enough, came to a dead end. In a time before dead ends became a threat and missing kids were seen on milk cartons, it used to be a lost world of high grasses and harmless snakes. I used to get lost among the pussy willows and cattails. I'd stand up on my toes and break them off midstem and bring them home to my mother for her pottery.

In our basement there were knots in the wood of the cabinets, which formed strange ghostlike characters when you looked at them for a long time. If I went down alone at night, I would be terrified.

I am sleepwalking late at night, past my parents' bedroom, where they are watching television with my brother Dan. I suppose I am being very quiet, because they don't hear me. When I wake, I'm standing in the basement next to the Kenmores, underneath the long string that turns on the bare light bulb overhead. I start to scream and cannot believe I am down here alone with the cabinets in the total darkness.

On Thanksgiving and Christmas, we'd take a sackful of groceries to Fanny Wimms at the old folk's home. She had been our maid before I was born. There were pictures of her in our family albums. She always looked seventy. "Praise Jesus, thank the dear Lord in heaven that my wonderful friends never forgot me—oh, Lord, they don't forget this poor old soul." She'd look at me in my little snowsuit, under those ugly winter Michigan skies, Fanny, with a few teeth missing, stroking my head. We'd send her back in from the cold, stockings bagging at the knees. She'd wave from behind the screen door, smiling.

CHILDHOOD FEARS

Brain damage from airplane glue
Fixative sprayed on chalk drawings
Bleach
Spiders
Mushrooms

My mother going blind from staring at an eclipse of the sun while I'm away at camp in Fenton, Michigan. And when I come home she has become an old woman and my father is pushing her around in a wheelchair and she doesn't remember who I am.

My friend Joanie had the cutest brother, a tiny little kid named Mike. Their mother had been in and out of institutions and was very high-strung. When we played cowboys and Indians at Joanie's house, I was a sheriff, and we put her mother—"the pretty little gal"—in jail, behind some swinging doors leading into the kitchen. Joanie would start to cry hysterically, and we'd have to let her mom out of jail.

We all walked home from the primary units one day, Joanie and Mike and I, we were five and he was three. He was wearing cowboy boots, and on the corner of Concord Street I pulled them off and then spanked him, accusing him of the deed. I held him and comforted him as he cried, and I helped him back on with his boots. But I kept doing it over and over. Joanie was hysterical, Mike was terrified, and finally my mother, who saw it all from our house, ran out and grabbed me, screaming, "What are you doing!" I looked down at the ground and told her I didn't know. Reassuring Joanie and Mike, she sent them home. I had to stay inside for the rest of the night to figure out what I had done.

My boyfriend Johnny was over after school and had a bladder problem. I pulled his pants down in the basement bathroom. He had the cutest penis I'd ever seen. I kept opening the door and laughing at him, and he couldn't pee. I wanted to touch it, it looked so tiny and soft. We played for a long time and he kept peeing and I went in and looked each time.

A spider crawled through a crack in the door.
I sat there and watched it walk across the floor.
It made me so sad I had to cry,
when it spun a web and began to fly.
It brought up a million memories,
of licking off a scabby knee,
of standing tiptoe so I could see
something far away that was bigger than me.

The first Hanukkah I can really picture is the one when I wanted a sparkle paint set and got it. We all were given a different present every night—little things that my mom kept up in the closet in my parent's room. Downstairs, a Christmas tree made out of aluminum, in blue and silver, just sort of sat there with no particular life of its own.

At night we lit the Hanukkah candles and I would sing the prayer I had just learned in Hebrew school. I went there after regular school on Tuesdays and Thursdays, listening to the Beatles on the way in cars driven by different mothers with fresh hairdos. There would be a snack of plain sugar cookies with a big sticky blob of strawberry jelly in the middle, which I would pull out and eat, sometimes discarding the rest of the cookie. For the next hour and a half I would feel nervous and hungry.

There was a period when everything I wore started to taste good. I used to sit in Hebrew school and suck on the sleeve of this one blue dress: it tasted salty but very satisfying. I had a yellow terry-cloth bathrobe, a hand-me-down from my brother David. I would pull out the threads and chew and swallow them while watching T.V. This became a favorite habit.

One day, taking a poop, I noticed that "it" was not really coming out but felt suspended over the water. I began to panic: was I shitting out my insides? After weeks of working their way through my colon, the terry-cloth threads were emerging—much to my horror and fear. Needless to say, the psychological implications were deep; I ·never told anyone. And I never ate my clothes again, no matter how delicious they looked.

When I was seven, I attended school at the Mackinaw Primary Units. My brothers had gone there too, and had the same teachers. The classrooms were all small houses with their windows painted in different pastels depending on the grade. My second-grade teacher, Irene Rolof, a spinster from Indiana, used to fall asleep during the reading lesson. All the teachers were old, except the occasional "teacher in training."

I used to have a recurring fantasy that I was being tortured by these teachers, kind of sexually. They would tie me up and do incantations and weird dark things. My mother would have to come and save me. It would be all these old hags against my mom; they would be naked and shoot milk out of their breasts into her eyes to try and blind her, but she always prevailed.

Everyone was throwing stones in the fresh cement behind the primary units. The builders, burly guys who didn't work for GM, were getting annoyed. "Who's throwin' them stones?" Lenny, a boy I loved, pointed his finger at me: "Sandy's doing it." The construction worker grabbed my little arm through the chain-link fence and started yelling at me. "If you was my little girl, I'd beat you black and blue!" All the kids were watching; I felt so humiliated. That smirk on Lenny's face all the years could not erase, even when he gave me a Carole King album on a visit to Flint after we moved to Arizona.

Kay Kay and I swore every morning on the way to school, every obscenity we knew.

I went home for lunch from the primary units and pretended my mother was a waitress in a roadside café. "I'll have a side order, ma'am"—a chunk of white-meat tuna, carrot strips, potato chips and a dollop of mayonnaise. And then I'd sit at the counter and ignore her.

I would clean out the ashtrays, dumping them into a silent butler my grandmother had bought my mother for these occasions. My mother served stuffed mushroom caps and Reese's smoked oysters on colored toothpicks.

Naomi was there in a sequined blue chiffon dress, and her diamond initial pinkie ring. A black couple mingled with the crowd, a doctor and his wife. She broke her heel off on the stairs up the "split level" and it gave her a migraine, so they left early. Milt and his wife, Marlene, were there also; he was my dad's partner. They belonged to the Willow Wood Country Club, where she would sit nursing an iced coffee for hours, wearing eggcup eye protectors and frying in Bain de Soleil. My parents wouldn't join the country club; my mother, being an artist, thought it was pretentious. It's because of that I never had a nose job and consequently became the girl I wanted to be.

Mott's was making a new applesauce, some with pineapple chunks in it, some with strawberries; they had new labels that really caught your eye. My mom and I bought several jars at the A & P. Along with a scoop of cottage cheese and some cold spaghetti, I ate almost an entire jar of strawberry applesauce. Afterward, I played for a while with our Boston terrier, Tinkerbell, on the steps in our split level, then I walked back to school.

By the time I arrived, I'd become incredibly sick to my stomach, and just outside the third-grade primary unit, I lost my bizarre lunch on the blacktop next to the crocuses. Fortunately I'd arrived a bit early, so most of the kids weren't there yet. Miss Brubaker, in a Kennedy-era tight skirt and heels—I had a major crush on her—was there and took out the lawn hose and washed it down into the bushes. I walked around sheepishly, explaining that the combination of what I ate didn't seem to digest very well, and wasn't Miss Brubaker great for cleaning it all up. Miss Brubaker was Mrs. Eckstrom's teaching assistant, and the whole incident was discussed when Mrs. Eckstrom returned in her Buick. We'd say Mrs. Eckstrom's favorite phrase—"the whole kit 'n' kaboodle"—every day in our best Walter Brennan voices.

Miss Rolof used to beat the pants off Jimmy Jones, a cute little boy with a speech impediment and a generic name. She whacked his ass until snot came flying out of his nose. "You have to learn to read!" she screamed. Now he spends most of his time reading Plath and Kafka.

Jackie Schaffer pulled a chair out from under me and I fell on my coccyx.

I learned to play "Hail, Hail, the Gang's All Here" on my ukelele. My father played "Slaughter on Tenth Ave" on his new stereo. Grammy Allen let me stay up until ten to see *Once Upon a Mattress* with Carol Burnett. Throughout the special, I could hear Grammy talking on the phone to Kate Monroe, telling her that she didn't think it was right, but it wasn't her place to say so.

My mother made ceramic totem poles and tiles for our new patio. At Flint Junior College, she became obsessed with anything Japanese. She had a tokonoma installed in the entry to our house, across from a small mirror framed by bleached oak, in which I had stared at my cheek, swollen from the mumps. During a fever-induced hallucination, alligators had crawled off my slippers and up the side of my parents' bed. My dad rubbed me down with alcohol and gave me a shot. I slept with them and watched *The Gale Storm Show* as I fell asleep.

My mother was wearing slippers and came out with two bottles of milk for my picnic in the backyard. She tripped and fell down, shattering the bottles and cutting her wrist. I was crying hysterically, and my brother Dan helped her up, all pale and with blood dripping down her hand. He called up my dad at the office and asked what to do. Staying really calm, he ran her hand under the kitchen faucet and then wrapped a towel tightly around her wrist. All my friends wanted to come in and look, but we sent them home with sandwiches.

I used to have this friend named David Cremens. I nicknamed him "Chinamoona," because he looked kind of Chinese with his moon-shaped face, but I think it was really because he was kind of poor white trash. I remember the time his mother threw a joint birthday party for him and his sister. All the kids had to sit two per chair, and she served pimento-loaf sandwiches, and peanut M & M's with milk. It was the saddest birthday party I ever went to.

In winter, his nose would always run, and he'd wipe it off on the back of his hand and his sleeve. Together we would chase girls, with worms on sticks.

At Christmas, everyone at the Mackinaw Primary Units would pick a name out of a hat to buy a gift for. You were always afraid someone creepy would get your name. That happened to me a few times, and I'd end up with an ugly plastic purse or a Tinkerbell perfume set, while other people would get great things like an Etch-A-Sketch or a new Barbie or Ken set—something really fun. If you got a lousy gift, you really couldn't say anything because maybe the family was poor and could barely afford what they did get you. It was all out of balance and embarrassing and someone was bound to run out crying and I would love it in a way.

Everyone would buy something for the teacher. She got a lot of bottles of perfume that the mothers didn't want, or some scarves, or maybe some nice costume jewelry—a Christmas tree pin or a jolly Santa Claus sweater holder, the kind that had clasps and holds the sweater lightly open.

Then we would have some potato latkes that "someone's mother was nice enough to make for all of us, so enjoy them and thank Jill for bringing them in." And we would light the candles to show all the Gentiles what a traditional Hanukkah was like. This would get me all excited.

When we let out for the vacation, even at seven, there was that nostalgic sentimental feeling that would continue for all the years of school.

I sat in the basement watching TV and applying a thin layer of Elmer's Glue-All over the palm of my hand. I would peel it off in one piece. I liked the way it smelled, kind of milky.

My dad came downstairs. Seeing me, he warned, "Are you sniffing that glue? Well, I sure hope you never sniff airplane glue."

"No, I never would," I said beginning to panic. "It can give you brain damage!"

That night in bed, I kept thinking: "Is this what it's like to have an empty mind? I felt all the thoughts in my head rushing out, like air from a balloon. I pinched myself, went into the bathroom and stared in the mirror, tried desperately to remember songs from various Broadway musicals I always sang, and finally I walked into my parents' room to let them know I had brain damage.

I wanted to see if I could sleep the whole night with a piece of gum in my mouth. It was a stick of Wrigley's Spearmint. I woke at 3 A.M. My hair was all tangled. "Mom, wake up! Help, I have bees in my hair!" We stood in the bathroom with the door closed, and she cut the gum out of my hair with a pair of cuticle scissors.

"Tornado" blankets were kept in a chest of drawers in the basement. Whenever there were storm warnings, we would go down and sit for hours, with everything unplugged. We would listen to the portable radio and wait for the storm to pass. My father would go outside and watch the funnel roar down the street, and then he'd come back inside to tell us about it. I would wrap myself in the tornado blanket in the dark.

Before 1955, the year I was born, there was never a tornado in Flint. In 1956, the first one hit on the outskirts of town in the middle of the night. People said it was like an explosion. In *National Geographic,* they showed photos of a twister just before it touched down randomly. I would stare at it for hours. In the encyclopedia, there was a photograph of a bolt of lightning that looked like a tall, skinny man walking across the sky.

When they announced a tornado warning at school and told us we had to go home right away, I couldn't move. I said I'd forgotten my way home, so they had to call my dad's office. He sent one of his nurses, a sexy blonde, over to pick me up. She seem annoyed but had to pretend to be nice about it. She must have been thinking what a weird, neurotic little kid I was.

I watched the first tablet of Salvo disintegrate in the washer. The Daunts, who were originally from Belgium, were throwing a party to celebrate a detergent that had been compressed into a giant tablet. It was comforting to see so much compacted into so little.

Cookies, coffee and milk were served in the recreation room as we waited to examine the results—the whitest and brightest we'd ever seen. We were all quiet and melancholy on the short drive home.

Mark and I watched the snowfall from his bedroom. He was lying on his bed, reading a rocket book by Wernher von Braun (whom he did a great impression of). We talked about space and going there. The bedspreads on the twin beds in his room were patterned with an array of explorers' ships. I would look down at the ancient boats and think how far we had come and where we had yet to go. We listened to the radio and heard a Supremes song that had just come out, maybe "Baby Love" or "Stop in the Name of Love." At that moment the universe seemed within grasp.

I was spending the night with Kay Kay, talking in the family dining room with Naomi, her mom, who wore a diamond initial pinkie ring, which she told me she'd got out of a Cracker Jack box—it was one of the really good prizes. Their maid, Annie, who was part of the family, made fried chicken. Everyone fought over the giblets and the hearts. The twins, Sandy and Andy, wore Beatles boots and never brushed their teeth. Harriet, the hot older sister, came home from a dance contest, proclaiming, "Look what your gorgeous talented daughter won in the dance contest! A Supremes forty-five!"

Harriet wanted my brother Mark's bleeding-madras jacket. Kay Kay and Harriet had their names in big, bold embroidery on their bedspreads, ate snacks in bed, and even had their own TV.

Marie played jazz piano. Tinkerbell, the Boston terrier, jumped up on her when she changed into her maid's uniform in the basement. I would poke her in the stomach as she stood in her bra and underpants next to the incinerator, the Kenmore washer and dryer, and the white-enamel electric range, which no one ever used. She came on Mondays, Wednesdays and Fridays, in a red Chevy Impala.

On holidays or days I stayed home sick, I'd follow her around the house and talk to her as she cleaned. Her husband had left her. Her son had drowned in the Flint River. She lived alone and drank a lot. I thought she looked part Indian. We drove her home once with our two birds which she'd take care of while we were out of town. My dad had bought a package of Limburger cheese. "Oh, my

God—put away that stinky stuff" she screamed when I opened it. I hugged her as she got out of the car.

When we came back from Detroit that Sunday, we sensed something was wrong when we walked through the back door—the house seemed too quiet. Upstairs, there were BBs from my father's closet scattered all over the floor. My mother's engagement ring, the only diamond she had, was missing.

Everyone immediately assumed that Marie had set us up. But there's no way it could be true.

When I was five, we went to Miami for Christmas. Everyone loaded up in the Pontiac station wagon and headed south. There was a time when Miami Beach was really great; I think that was one of the years it still was. Lying on the beach with the family, behind some pink hotel, I watched a Santa Claus in full gear walking up and down the beach, handing out dolls and guns to all the little Jewish kids. "Look at this putz!" some big, fat cigar-smoking guy named Manny is spouting off to his pal and their two wives, while I am wrapping a pink blanket around the naked baby. Later, I walk along the beach, picking up seashells.

I went to the 1965 World's Fair in 1964. I never understood that. What a feeling of awe to look up at the Unisphere and the gleaming rocket ships, at the pavilions, so colorful and international.

We stayed in a hotel that was built for the fair. On the night we checked in, we were awakened by the smell of acrid smoke. The hotel had been put up in such a hurry that the wiring was faulty and short-circuited in our part of the hotel. The manager, a very slick-looking guy in a dark suit, apologized profusely and gave us his apartment in the hotel. We looked through his album collection. He had all the Barbra Streisand records, and my brother Dan said he had really good taste, so I felt especially sophisticated staying in his suite.

I begged my dad to take us to see *Funny Girl* that summer—it was the hottest ticket in town—but he took us to see a matinee of *Any Wednesday*, with Sandy Dennis, instead. We said, "Let's go see a woman who is going to be doing the exact same thing for the next fifteen years," but she did it best in *Any Wednesday*, you have to admit.

That was Barbra Streisand's first big year, when she was "Simply Barbra," with the Egyptian eyeliner, long red fingernails, and pageboy. She sang songs like "Free Again": "Lucky, lucky me, free again!" Then she moved out to Hollywood and she went "down the stoney end"; she never wanted to go "down the stoney end," but someone forced her to crimp her hair and and go "down the stoney end." We miss you, Barbra. Come back to the five-and-dime, Barbra Streisand, Barbra Streisand.

I remember the day my mom and I were supposed to meet my brother and my father at the Indonesian Pavilion. I mean, who could remember Pavilion, let alone Indonesian. We spent the entire day looking for each other. There's something about being around all those people that makes you think you'll never see anyone you know, ever again. It was all such a new concept. No one speaks of pavilions anymore, and that saddens me somehow.

In the city, we stayed at a Howard Johnson's, and somehow a motor lodge in Manhattan was a perfect experience. My mom and I stood and looked out the window and watched what seemed to be a hundred fire trucks race by. The city never seemed to stop. Maybe Marilyn Monroe was there, studying with Lee Strasberg—the city had that kind of energy. No one ever went out without a suit and tie or a dress. Men had raincoats thrown over their arms, which seemed to stay in that position all the time. My mother had blond streaks running through her neat hairdo.

Now, on the way in from JFK to the city, I'll stare at what remains of the '65 World's Fair, the rockets burned out and crumbling, the Unisphere tarnished, and those fantastic rusted sculptural structures, with lights all around them to warn incoming jets. As I look back over my shoulder, I break down and weep over what could have been but was never meant to be.

She changed her name to Frosty* in the spring of '65. She drove her Chevy pickup to a midwestern town where a strong woman could get a decent job. She spent her nights in a rented garage with a single bed and a set of weights. She built up her arms, saved some money pumping gas and changing oil, found her dream in a little town with simple ways.

She found a "wife," Jeanelle,* who had two kids, Billy and Raelyn, from a previous marriage. Frosty treated them just great. She used Brylcream and bought Jeanelle a diamond ring and a tiny gold necklace with "Frosty" carved on its charm. Frosty liked her new name, and no one ever asked her what it used to be.

Frosty took a course in auto mechanics, and before long everyone was coming to her for busted crankshafts, worn break drums, burned-out alternators. Even the most macho truckdrivers listened to her advice, and she'd show them pictures of the kids. She'd be there at Lucky's 7 Eleven all-night service station until four in the morning. And Jeanelle would come by with a sack lunch, including a big piece of lemon meringue pie. Frosty, holding a monkey wrench, would smile and blow her a greasy kiss.

I was on a family vacation the summer someone put water in our gas tank, and we got stuck in this little town for three days. My dad ran all over talking to mechanics, and most of them were lazy and kept saying, "Go see Frosty. She's the only one who'll be able to help you out." I was intrigued as the tow truck pulled into her garage. She explained everything to my dad, and I kept getting this weird feeling in my stomach. I guess I sensed something. She made scary faces at me from under the hood and kept laughing and whispering, "Come here, I'll show you what's wrong!" I stood by my dad, shy and nervous. She talked about where she was from and how much she loved this little town and how there was some good fishing nearby and why didn't we rent one of her "junkers" and head on out to the lake. She gave us some worms and told my dad what a pretty wife he had. My mom was sitting on the Nehi machine, doing a sketch.

All that night, I kept waking up, hearing the sounds of trucks roaring by on the highway. I'd go into the bathroom to look in the mirror, because I felt that I was changing. I pulled up my pajamas, and I remember it was the first time I noticed my breasts. I felt these two hard bumps and started to panic. I wouldn't wake up my parents, so I left the light on and closed the door, except for a crack. I lay in bed, and Frosty's laugh and pompadour kept drifting into my head.

Before we left Flint for Arizona, my mother had a Japanese architect named Hanamora redesign the living room and dining room into an ultracontemporary shrine to the wishful thinking of the early sixties. She had the front entrance positioned to one side—a statement in itself—and painted a deep sky blue. It had a stainless-steel Scandinavian door handle, and the wood used was oak.

On a spring night, I closed the door on my middle fingernail. The next day my father heated up a needle with his lighter and poked a hole in the fingertip to let blood out and relieve the pressure. Many months went by before the nail grew, pushing the old nail out. We noticed it at Rosh Hashanah services, me and my dad: it smelled like ripe bananas. We sat sniffing it during the blowing of the shofar. When we went home, my dad cut back the old nail and it fell off, revealing the fresh new one underneath. I wrapped the dead nail carefully in a Kleenex and took it around the neighborhood, showing it to all the kids. To this day, the nail on that finger is different—wider, flatter and scarred.

We ate at Japanese restaurants all the way across the country, starting in Denver. My mom with her Oriental obsession discovered a slew of them along the route to Arizona. We nicknamed her the "shapes and forms" lady, for as we hit a terrain with mountains, she would cry out, "Oh, look at all those shapes and forms!" We ate more sukiyaki in one week than the average family in Tokyo. My mother went in a whole new direction in her art, influenced by the terrain and by Japanese food.

Moving from Flint to Phoenix meant giving up a beautiful home in a secure place. What, we all wondered, did my father have in mind, transplanting us to this alien world of red sunsets and people without roots?

We stayed in a cheap embarrassing bungalow on Seventh Street when we arrived in Phoenix. It was there that I first manifested an obsession and phobia about gas stoves. I had always read how people were asphyxiated by them or how easily they exploded and sent people flying through doors. So when I had to sleep on a foldaway couch in the living room, not far away from the stove, I kept waking myself up during the night to make sure there was no leak.

Positive that everyone was out to get me, I would pack my lunch every day in a brown paper sack, which I very carefully folded over and over, then stapled, then wrapped all around the top with freezer tape. Once I was at school, I kept an eye on it until lunchtime, when I would carefully examine it for any signs of tampering, such as needle holes where something could have been injected. If there was evidence that anything had been altered, I would throw out the entire lunch.

Diane Adler and I went to Christown almost every Saturday. Sometimes we'd go to a newer mall, called Los Arcos —The Arches. We'd take twenty, maybe thirty-five dollars, and somehow we would be able to find a new pair of hiphuggers at Chess King or a pot of lip gloss at Diamond's department store. There were so many places to shop for beaded Indian headbands, thick leather belts with big brass peace-sign buckles, a Moody Blues album. We'd check out the boys, mostly white trash, with greasy hair parted in the middle.

Diane and I were watching *The Odd Couple*, with Jack Lemmon and Walter Matthau, when I heard my mother's voice calling my name. It was a matinee at the Camelback Theater, and people were turning around to see what was going on. My mom had this frantic insane look on her face. Diane and I walked out into the lobby with her.

"Thank God I found you!" She was out of control.

41

"I can't believe you were screaming my name in the middle of *The Odd Couple*. You scared the hell out of me. What's going on?"

"Some girl who sounded just like you called me up and sounded really out of it. She must have been on drugs and kept saying, 'Mommy, help me, I don't know where I am, I'm really fucked up, help me,' so I got in the car and rushed over here as fast as I could. Oh, thank God you're all right; I had to be sure. Go ahead and finish the movie. I'll pick you up when it's over. Gee, I was so scared for you —it really sounded like you!"

Diane and I walked back to our seats, and I turned around to see my mom, in her lime-green stretch pants, standing and talking to the theater manager.

Diane and I were best friends. We went to our first concert together, Simon and Garfunkel. I wore a blue wool pleated skirt with a blue-yellow-and-white-striped turtleneck. We went to Hebrew school together and tortured Mr. Goldberg, our Hebrew teacher. We were outcasts of a sort and couldn't get any of the boys we thought were really cute, so we settled for boys we could push around, like Mike. Mike is probably very handsome now and wasn't so bad then. He liked me too much. The three of us got this old lady to buy us tickets for *The Night They Raided Minsky's*, with Elliott

Gould, which was rated "R." We got all excited because there was a flash of titty.

Afterward, outside Montgomery Ward, I pinned Mike up against the wall and tried to unzip his pants so we could see his penis. It really embarrassed him, and it made me feel angry. In Diane's father's van, Mike put his hands down my pants.

I wore Cachet. I kept the bottle displayed on the bathroom counter at home as if it were my own apartment, decorated with Parsons tables and modular furniture, with the latest *Cosmo* tossed casually next to my foldout couch. I spent hours in the bathroom, steaming my face and waiting for my period to start.

My mom sent away for the Kotex learner's kit, which included big pads and a belt for the napkin, and all kinds of information about menstruation. I kept it under the sink, where it collected dust in the fading pink box. By the time I finally started my period, in November of my senior year of high school, I'd forgotten all I had learned from my kit and used tampons.

Who did I like more, Jessie or Brian? I would sit for hours in Jessie's room, taking the *Cosmopolitan* tests with her. I'd ask her the questions and mark her answers with a pencil in the little spaces provided. I'd pose them in seductive ways, baiting her to give the sexiest response. Jessie had long, dark hair. She reminded me of Susan Dey from the Partridge Family; her brother Brian was slightly effeminate and reminded me of David Cassidy, who played Keith Partridge. We'd go on long bike rides. One afternoon, Brian called and invited me to a movie, but my mother said, "Absolutely not." I was crushed—I think that's the last time anyone asked me out on a date.

They lived next door, and at night I could see Brian's shadow as he undressed. I wished sometimes that I could climb through his window and touch him. They moved away so suddenly that I never found out where they went on to. That's the way Arizona was, kind of like thumbing through a magazine, looking at the pictures, then having somebody throw it out before you ever got to read the stories.

They were such a romantic family, and somehow I felt left out. Undoubtedly there was a tragedy waiting right around the corner that would bring them even closer together, holding back the tears, being strong and brave for Father, because that's the way he would have wanted it—it was the kind of thing that made you envious of someone else's pain. Sad things happened only to other people, and usually they were Gentile.

Mindy wore days-of-the-week underpanties: Monday's on Wednesdays, Sunday's on Tuesdays—she could afford to be that carefree. She was a perfect blonde and the new kid in town. It was a fluke that Mindy took to me. Like some Muse, I made her laugh. Her mother, who was much younger than her father, would take us shopping in Scottsdale in their big white Cadillac convertible.

I'd sing in my best voice, songs like "Leaving on a Jet Plane." Mindy and her mother seemed enthralled. I'd pretend to be interested in the football player Mindy had a crush on, or in how she had "made out" with Kurt Russell when he was a Disney star, in the stable where her horse was kept in Denver; her mother really wanted them to get married someday. I kept staring at a small mole Mindy had on the side of her nose. We didn't stay friends after our freshman year, but she was always nice to me when she saw me, even if she was walking hand in hand with her football player boyfriend.

I remember myself glued to the TV in someone's La-Z-Boy recliner, engaging in the fantasies of a fourteen-year-old baby-sitter. Saturday night, the "art" station in Phoenix showed movies like *The Virgin Spring. Playbody After Dark* had sexy extras providing atmosphere and guests like Lenny Bruce's mom. Cocktails and big breasts abounded. I wondered how long it would take me to get there. Love, American style, was so relevant, insightful and timely. It was painful for me to search through the drawers of the people I baby-sat for, looking for signs of sex, nasty little things that shot images of unsexy people having sex.

KDKB played underground music—the Moody Blues, Jimi Hendrix, Janis Joplin, The Doors, Cream, some classical stuff, and then a touch of jazz. I would lie in my bedroom with its astrological wallpaper in blues, purples and greens, and rest my head on the Indian-print bedspread and pillows I had bought at a head shop that smelled like incense, and Joni Mitchell would come pouring out of the cheap speakers as if she were right there in the canyon chatting with me, about Trina and her wampum beads, and the priest who sat in the airport bar, about Willy, who was her child and her father and all her various lovers. I, too, thought about love and all the interns who would come and go, staying right across the hall as guests in our house, all drenched in Aramis and wearing shirts with big collars and wide ties.

They would come from Chicago or Detroit and swim in the hot sun in tight-crotched bathing suits. I would go out there all excited and skinny in some semblance of a bikini, and I'd talk to them as if we were all at a cocktail party. Scared of the deep water, I'd stay in the shallow end, getting splashed in the face and looking stupid. Later in the day, we would take turns in the bathroom, showering. I'd listen at the door, wishing I could just walk in naked and rub up against them and have them really want me. Dressed in a granny gown, I would go out with my parents for dinner, and the two interns would go out too.

Late at night, I would lie in bed and hear them come in, talking quietly and laughing. "Great tits," I'd hear, and "Too bad we have to head back." "Maybe I'll do my residency here after all." "Just to get laid?" "I've done crazier things than that to get a little hot pussy." What about me? I'm fourteen and alone here. I've got a great bedroom, with Parsons tables and a Campbell's Soup trash can.

On Sunday, after bagels and lox, my dad and I would take them to the airport and drop them off. They would shake hands with my dad and give me a kiss on my cheek. Look, as far as I'm concerned, don't ever fucking come back here, because by then you'll be wanting me and I'm not going to be in the least bit interested.

Jim worked in a Texaco station at Lake Louise, Canada, next to the little lodge we stayed in, owned by a patient of my dad's. Jim was handsome and sexy. I watched him from my room as he pumped gas in an olive-drab uniform with a red Texaco star. He had a chipped front tooth and he smelled like fresh gasoline and sweat. I was fourteen, at my sexual peak. He took me and my father out trout fishing on the lake. What an incredible sight he was, carrying the oars with such power and authority! He rowed us around the lake, telling stories, putting bait on my hook, bringing in the fish. I smiled at him and carried on an adult conversation.

I lay awake all night, hoping he'd come in and make love to me. I finally fell asleep as the sun came up.

I carried around a picture of him I'd taken; he was leaning against the gas pump. I didn't see him again until three or four years later. He was living in Vancouver then and working for a petroleum company. He had lost his intensity and was now shorter than I. When he took us out fishing, he was always out of breath, and I noticed how fat he had become. When we were alone, Jim tried to kiss me.

I felt bad that I didn't want him anymore. That night I lay in bed staring at his old picture.

We were leaving for Las Vegas that morning. I was so excited about spending the Christmas holidays amid the glitz and glamour that I could have burst. My brother Mark woke up with strep throat and a fever. I stood in the hallway pacing and gritting my teeth, as my father took his temperature. I kept thinking: Damn it, he's going to ruin another vacation. Somebody always does this! Then I thought: He's going to be fine—he'll feel better as soon as we pack up the car. But as the morning wore on, Mark got worse, developing this white pus thing on his arm. I hated him that day. We ended up just hanging around, which nobody seemed to mind except me.

I made my mother buy this black-and-white-striped mini-dress. She looked strangely beautiful in it. The first time she wore it was right after Mark smoked grass at home, had an allergic reaction and flipped out. This whole thing came down about my two older brothers turning him on to it and how they both had experimented with a lot of other drugs. My dad was in the middle of tying his tie, one I had picked out at Saks; it was striped pink. He was looking in the bathroom mirror when my mother threw herself on the bed, with the obligatory "Why me? What did I do wrong? I feel so damn bad."

I stood for a minute watching her and listening for my dad's reaction. "For Christ's sake! You act like we're responsible. They're goddamn ingrates. What do you expect?" I walked over to the bed, and leaning over her, I started to yell, "You get hold of yourself right now, little lady. This is ridiculous!" I had such authority. After a few minutes, she became calm and got up. I smoothed her minidress, and she hugged me, her eyelids swollen. "You're right," she said. I looked at her and touched her face and said, "It's going to be all right. Now have fun at the party and bring me something back. If I'm asleep, wake me up. You both look great. Have fun."

I cleaned the kitchen that night, something I would do a lot on Saturdays. I would soap the avocado-green kitchen counter and wash it down, wipe the sugar and flour containers, the top of the GE toaster-oven, the built-in stove's top. I made it my own home. My husband was out for the evening.

Our swivel color TV would be on in the background, with Mary Tyler Moore, and our English bulldogs would walk in and out and I'd talk to them. "Hey, mama, what are you doing? Come here and let me talk to you!" I'd go get a pair of my brother's old underpants and make CoCo wear them until she struggled out. "No, honey, you've got to wear these because you look very pretty, pretty baby girl—yes, you are *so* pretty!" I talk to lovers that way now and think about how cute CoCo was when I dressed her up.

When I finished cleaning up the kitchen, I would have a bowl of Smitty's Big Town chocolate ice cream, mushed up with milk. I would fall asleep during *The Wild Wild West*, with Robert Conrad as James West and Ross Martin as Artemus Gordon. I noticed that although *The Wild Wild West* was supposed to take place in the 1800s, all the women wore sixties eyeliner.

On Sunday mornings I would make rounds with my dad. On those drives out to the hospital, he would confide in me about everything that was going on in his life. Things were falling apart with the doctor he was partners with: "Oh, Christ, he's a real schmuck. He's a real selfish guy.

"Your brothers are a bunch of goddamn ingrates! Always thinking of their good times; that's all that matters to them—good times!"

A tumbleweed would fly by, a cold desert breeze would blow in the window, as I listened and nodded in agreement.

"I can't tell your mother about this, because she'll throw it up in my face. You know her. She's got those abstract ideas. She's just not practical, always collecting all that junk. It drives me nuts!"

I sat next to him, the man who was the hero of my life, who could do no wrong, could figure out everything, was compassionate with his patients, a friend to all those frightened people, answering calls in the middle of the night. I remember hearing him through the whole house, calmly answering people's questions about fevers, chest pains, stomach cramps and sore throats. He'd get up at 5 A.M. and make toast with blueberry jam by Smucker's spread on it and eat an entire sunny-side-up egg in one bite.

Granny dresses, peplum skirts, iris eye shadow, green velour pullovers, thin-striped nylon knee socks, fringe scarves as thick as marshmallows, and derelict broken-down platform boots—the accoutrements of Saguaro High School. Mary wore them; Kimmy pulled them off for gym, stoned on pot, humming something from "Ladies of the Canyon," with dirty hair; Paula kept them on during basketball and took a trip to the principal to figure out what had happened to her tennis shoes. We watched her walk through the parking lot, looking back over her shoulder, flipping the bird and laughing with her head thrown back. Our gym teacher, with streaked shoulder-length hair, stood defiantly, hands on hips, flaunting her engagement ring and staring back at Paula, making sure she kept walking in the right direction.

I was good at archery, fell off the balance beam, hid out during tumbling and dodgeball, where we were encouraged to throw the ball at Janine, a shy girl with a big growth on her cheek, all veiny and red: "easy target, fast points"— that was the concept. I stood back with Stacey, with her thick Rasta strawberry-blond hair and acid flashbacks, feeling bad but not showing it. Janine, leaning a few feet away on a tetherball pole, held in her humiliation and tears. Stacey shrugged her shoulders and turned away. I smiled and waved.

In creative writing class, taught by Miss Messmer—we called her "Messmer-eyes" because of her thick glasses—Stacey showed me the watch she had stolen from the drugstore. I got up in front of the class and lectured about the dangers of pot smoking and irresponsibility: "No one cares anymore, Stacey stole this watch and thinks it's cool, you're all stoned, or too rich and spoiled to see what's going on in the world, and it's all going to come back to haunt you!" Stacey stood up and said, "Thanks a lot, asshole. That's the last time I ever trust anyone again!" Miss Messmer stared at us in disbelief. She didn't say anything. She was too frightened of us. We tortured her for walking kind of hunched over and those glasses and her oily hair and gawky legs. She was, however, the only teacher who ever recognized any talent in me and always wrote important notes on my assignments that encouraged me.

ONE SUNDAY REMEMBER

I wrote this story for creative writing class at Saguaro High, my junior year. Miss Messmer's comment read: "What impresses me most about this story is your fine control of subjects you have a stake in. A most impressive story —please let me have a copy before the year is out."

They always called me a "blithe spirit," and being a magmanimos human being, I usually gave them, more than I received.

I usually get up at 7:30 in the morning, the first thing I do is jump out of bed, stub my toe, and throw open my curtains and stare magnetically into the bay, and on any Sunday morning it seems the fog is melted early and San Francisco is mirrored off the ocean and it prisms into my bedroom, on Sundays it makes me sleepy, on workdays it usually more than not makes me late for work.

I like to daydream, while I eat my hot Cream of Wheat my stereo resounds softly in the background, somehow the Livines always hear it and he raps my ceiling with an umbrella.

I turn it off.

I scramble into the "john" and thoughtfully

55

brush my teeth, always making sure the incisors are "bright, white." I weigh myself, thank god, still 89 pounds.

Everybody at the office kids me, "uh oh here comes spaghetti legs, stand clear." But I laugh because I know their big jokers, I always laugh, ha, ha.

I can't find the rest of it.

I worked one summer in Central Supply, wrapping surgical equipment for sterilization. My two co-workers, Vi and Jeanette, taught me the fine points of wrapping the various instruments in the special trays; they knew it inside out. Each day I would look at the schedule of surgery to be done, simple procedures: tonsillectomies, appendectomies, clitorectomies. Once in a while some ambitious, daring surgeon would decide to do a major operation, like a coronary bypass, and the hospital, which was small, would be buzzing with excitement. The scrub nurses came marching in with arrogant attitudes, ordering up unusual implements and treating Vi and Jeanette like dirt. They were nicer to me because my father was a doctor. I'd stand around in my greens and my surgical shower cap, hair all tucked up underneath, looking like a goon, trying to flirt with the

When my parents were first married, they would stay up late, eating butter-and-onion sandwiches and having fun.

Dave was the most excited when I was born; he told everyone at school. Dan and Mark were cautious.

"When I was just a little girl, I asked my mother, 'What would I be? Would I be pretty? Would I be rich?' Here's what she said to me..."

Sandra next to a young Saguaro.

Measuring a brain for experimental purposes.

A Beanie copter from the "Beanie & Cecil" era.

I used to make CoCo wear my brother's underpants.

*C*ontemporary life in Scottsdale, AZ.

*B*oba wore wigs and told us how she danced on the big stages in Moscow. She wrote a book called Such a Life, published when she was in her eighties. It was a Book-of-the-Month Club selection, and was favorably reviewed by Mario Puzo.

My brother Dan would sit in the basement listening to Bob Dylan.

My dad's mom Lillian bought my mother a silent butler for a big cocktail party.

I *used to cut my grandfather's fingernails for him and brush the sides of his hair.*

podiatry residents, asking questions about bunions and spurs as I removed my cap, revealing a limp shag hairdo.

"Bye bye, Miss American Pie, Drove my Chevy to the levee but the levee was dry . . ." "Don't change it; I love this song." I put my hand over Daniel's, which was poised to change the station to something classical. I picked Daniel and Tom up every morning in my aqua '63 Dodge Polara and drove us all to Saguaro High. ("Go Sabercats Go!") They were my two best friends in high school, the only ones I trusted. In the winter, the windshield would freeze over and I'd drive blindly to Dan's, with Tom in the back-seat, covering his eyes. I'd scream at Dan to bring out a pot of hot water to throw on the glass. Invariably I was late and in one of those bad moods. I'd tear up Pima Road so fast that one time I did a hundred-ninety-degree spin into a ditch and back onto the road without missing a beat, in my Ultrasuede midicoat and with my two best friends laughing hysterically in utter amazement.

It was a ritual with us every day after school our senior year to go back to my house and eat salads with garbanzo beans and watch *Lost in Space*, with Dr. Smith and Will Robinson. Later in the afternoon, we'd ride our bikes around the mountains, through country clubs, and I'd lament that I wanted to go to the St. Luke's Hospital ball, with girls like Suki Kitchell. I would take both Dan and Tom as my dates. I never knew how much they both cared about me.

On long walks after dinner, with Tom's dog, Misty, running alongside us, rooting around cactuses, we talked about escaping this unimaginative, mundane desert life and heading to exotic places and having affairs with beautiful people. "I'd like to rape Sloane in the backseat of my Dodge after a Phoenix Suns game one night. I'll invite her to go and then throw her in the back and do it, just completely blow her mind." I'd say things like that with total conviction, and Dan would laugh so loud it echoed in the hills.

Tom was a hiker and wanted us to join the Sierra Club and put my hiking boots to good use. Dan was going to L.A. in November to catch the New York City Opera, with Beverly Sills. He'd stay with his cousin Jack and Jack's artist friend John in Pasadena; they lived this incredibly smart life that we all envied and dreamed about. On Friday nights, while everyone else was showing school spirit at football games, we would drive around Scottsdale in Dan's orange Camaro. On the way to see *The Garden of the Finzi-Continis*, we listened to *Don Giovanni*, with Joan Sutherland. Tom in the back, I'd get in the front, wearing too much Estée Lauder perfume, and talk in a big voice about how I didn't get the solo in chorus, maybe letting out a sharp operatic note for effect.

I made Daniel buy a salmon-colored Yves Saint Laurent suit with a vest for some important evening at the opera; the suit shrank after the first dry cleaning. Tom, with his curly thick hair, his T-shirts and bell-bottom jeans and hiking boots, and Daniel, tall and elegant, and I, with a face I had yet to grow into, were caught in a flash flood on the way home from a Cat Stevens concert, and landed at Dan's brother's place, where we sat talking to him and his girlfriend Debra. My dad finally came in our Chevy van and told the police out on Shea Boulevard we had to get home; we had bulldogs and they couldn't be left alone. I was so proud of him for getting us through.

Whenever Dan called, my father would get this disgusted look on his face and scream, "Your friend Dan is on the phone. For Christ sake, that kid talks so loud!" We spent every day together from the minute we met in Miss Sarapata's English class, right after I had reenacted giving birth from a sex-education film. Tom moved next door in my junior year. The three of us hooked up and never did anything without each other. If I could still have it that way I would. Somehow it always flowed, and there was an unspoken understanding among us about our desires and our pain.

I graduated half a year before them and left for a kibbutz in Israel. Both of them were going to meet me in June, but only Dan ended up coming. Our triad kind of fell apart after that; Dan and I became more bonded than ever. I screamed at him the day he arrived in Israel. I was cold and distant, and he told me how much he loved me. I couldn't handle it—I never could when anyone really loved me. By the time we got to Greece, we began to know each other and understand. But I missed Tom sometimes, his quiet funniness, his stamina and inner strength. If ever there was a time to be a freak without regret, it was then, with our dreams so close to the bone and our hearts pure. Often I go back to the memory of the nights we walked for hours in a still-undeveloped neighborhood, those silent desert nights cut in places by the sound of laughter and low-toned secrets between young friends.

My grandmother—we called her Boba—would always say, "I want to dance at your wedding!" Tonight I talked to my mother, who's visiting her in Michigan. She doesn't remember most of the family anymore. Mom told me she bought her a cute outfit at Kmart, pink slacks and a candy-cane-striped blouse with a pink sweater. Boba turned up the collar and said it looked real sharp. She wore wigs for years, different shades of blond; she would tell Mom to wear them too.

I used to sit on my twin bed and talk to her while she put on her makeup by the window—she liked the natural light. She'd tell me romantic stories about Russia, big rambling epics that could go on as long as her visit.

At night, she would scratch my back until it turned red, and we'd talk for hours, falling asleep. Right before I dozed off, she'd say, "I love you, mama zeze." "I love you too, mama zeze." She had a bridge with two teeth in it; she kept it by the sink at night and I'd find it in the morning. I would smell the different face lotions she'd use twice a day, smacking under her chin with the back of her hands and stroking her cheeks to "chase away the wrinkles." She taught me all her beauty secrets; a woman should always look her best around the men.

She's in some home now with mostly Gentiles. If they play music, she'll roll up her pants and dance like she did "on the big stages in Moscow." Sometimes I think about the silky Chinese pajamas she liked to wear, in odd shades of coral or aqua; I remember her shuffling around in her slippers, doing her morning stretches without fail, pulling on her special corset, her slacks ensemble, and always her wig.

Around ten-thirty or eleven in the morning she would appear and have her cup of coffee and piece of toast with cottage cheese, and she and my mom would speak Yiddish in low tones about my father or my "Zeyde," her husband, who was the bane of her existence. Maybe during the day other relatives would drop by—Aunt Bessie if she happened to be in town, or some distant cousin from a town near Minsk. Sometimes we'd go to Diamond's department store and buy panties or some hiphuggers from Chess King and then go back to Diamond's "tearoom" for lunch. On the way out, we'd maybe buy special face powder or a new stick of eye shadow. When we got home, I'd unwrap everything and show it to my dad for his approval.

On holy days I try to include almost everyone I know in my prayers. They are simple ones, my hopes for the survival of the world and mankind in general.

I used to rehearse the "four questions" at Passover during the afternoon before the seder. I would sing them over and over, knowing that usually I would be the youngest, the asker of the questions. For most of my life, my grandfather led the service, rattling off the Haggadah, rapid-fire. The women would talk, going back and forth to the kitchen to make sure nothing burned. They spoke in loud whispers, my grandmother, the aunts, the cousins, chattering away. My brothers would be getting high on Mogen David, and intermittently one of them would tell the women to be quiet. My grandmother would just wave them off, laugh, and keep on talking.

At the holidays, whenever relatives came to visit at home, I would forget the feeling of desolation that often overcame me. Many nights I would fall asleep with the sounds of older great-aunts and uncles and distant cousins murmuring in Yiddish. One night, I woke up out of a sound sleep with a stomachache. My mom's cousin Jerry from Detroit, the podiatrist, was downstairs. He gave me some literature and x-rays of feet, and I sat on the toilet listening to them talk and holding the x-rays up to the light.

I went to see *The Rocky Horror Show* at the Roxy thirteen times my first summer in L.A., the summer of '74. It was a big success as a play way before it became the Friday-night midnight classic. I got to know a lot of the other kids who hung out there; some had seen it sixteen times. I got invited to a few parties with the cast, at various houses in the Hollywood Hills.

One night I got a ride home with a French guy,

who turned out to be a parking attendant at the Rainbow. He started kissing me as we pulled away from the party and talked me into letting him come up. I was sharing my apartment with a bisexual guy I met in beauty school, who had built himself a tent in the living room with its green-and-blue shag carpet, and carried on with an assortment of creeps. The French guy slept next to me in the bedroom and the next morning insisted we have sex. There's nothing worse than a dry fuck with a stranger.

Two weeks went by, and I woke up with what I believe was the first case of herpes in L.A. I had to pour water over myself as I peed, it burned so bad. I cried to the doctor, who reprimanded me and told me I'd have to live with it. And I have, and have remained frighteningly faithful to a Frenchman I have never seen again.

I have what I would describe as a plunging V-neck depresssion.

I took a couple of acting classes my first years in L.A. We would meet on hot nights in a room with no air-conditioning. A bunch of waiters with hangovers and girls who sold makeup at Bullock's would lie on the floor doing relaxation exercises and deep breathing and letting go; that was always my favorite part.

I ran into Shirelle today at the Holiday Spa. I walked by her and knew immediately who she was. I didn't have good memories of her, so I kept walking; she did a double take and called me Sarah, which was reason enough to ignore her. We went to manicuring school together, the Charles Ross School of Beauty. There was nothing beautiful about it, believe me.

Shirelle is six feet tall, and black. She always wore her hair a quarter of an inch long. I'd give her a ride home every day to her apartment on Kings Road, which I never drive down anymore because everyone I know who lived on that street fucked me over. We'd sit in my car and talk for a long time about living in L.A. and people's sexual trips. It was my first summer on my own, and I lived with my aunt and uncle in Westwood. I ran around in six-inch wooden platform shoes with plastic fruit. Toward the end of manicuring class, I was hanging out with a bunch of gay hairdressers on Norton Avenue in West Hollywood, where I eventually moved, and Shirelle got kind of mean and gossipy about me and really cold. She thought I was a kook and doubted I'd amount to much of anything. She was only partially correct.

Every butch young guy in Levi's and a sweat-stained T-shirt had my attention. As "Rock the Boat" played on and on, I would get lifted high in the air. They would swing me around, with my bad haircut and plucked eyebrows, and dry hump me on the dance floor.

I had a big crush on one of them, a really silly photographer from England who had been married years before and had a kid somewhere. I used to sleep next to him on the floor of Joe's apartment on Norton before I moved in there. We would fall asleep to Barbra Streisand. We never fucked, with his uncut penis.

Joe was a hairdresser in Brentwood. He was short and bald and had a mustache. His really tight, sinewy body always smelled of Jōvan Musk. He had these pea-green sheets on his bed, which I know for a fact he never changed, because I used to study the stains and they never went away the entire summer I stayed there. He had a weird sissy voice and was obsessed with Streisand in a way I haven't seen since.

Those were very clear-cut times for homosexual men. The music, the extremes in sex and the lack of commitment to anyone in particular created an aura of constant fun and dark heat that I soaked up. I never touched it, I only heard it through walls, the strange sound of men inside men screaming, detached, breaking all the rules, taking to the extreme all those male things that get refined in heterosexuality.

He was not an ordinary boy from the San Gabriel Valley. His looks were deceiving, and he wanted out. He grew up in La Puente, with names of freeway exits, like Francisquito. It contained pockets of worn houses with four or five cars parked around the yard, scraps of bicycles, inner tubes, aluminum fishing boats and camper shells. Heavyset women stayed up late, bathed in the glow of the TV and surrounded by snacks.

Jack moved to Pasadena and worked as a bartender in a "happening" gay bar. He was funny and fast and drank too much. We stayed in touch over the years from the *Rocky Horror* Roxy days, when he'd hang out and I'd broil up some chicken breasts for dinner.

We had wild parties back then, when I first came to Los Angeles. He was one of my first friends—a kid who knew he was gay when he was fourteen. It was a curse, a misfortune and bad timing that my friend succumbed at a cruel and much too early age.

Cap sleeves and French sleeves were very big when I was a manicurist in Beverly Hills. Women wearing a lot of good jewelry and flared gabardine pants would come to the salon and sell T-shirts imported from France. The customers would get out their wallets and stand around asking questions about how to care for them and would go to the dressing room to try them on, usually stretching them out of shape and blaming someone else when they didn't end up buying them. I could see them in there with their cleavages and freckles, applying lipstick in the mirror. I bought one with cap sleeves that made my arms appear so long I looked like a Gumby; I never wore it again.

There were three manicurists at the salon. I was the youngest. One of the others was Indonesian, very exotic and bitchy. She treated me like a kid. She was a real hustler. Dyan Cannon was always inviting her over to her house in

Malibu. I'd sit a few seats away and listen in on these women talking in innuendo. I did Dyan one time when Indo was away, and she never looked at me as I dug sand from under her big toenail.

There was this big blonde who used to come in; she had really bad hair and added pieces to make it look thicker. Indo did her too. She was divorced from some Hollywood type but still had some connections. She was always going to parties and telling about this "fag" and that "dyke." Her story was that she had come to L.A. from Ohio and got a job as a meter maid in Bev Hills. That's how she met her husband. She ended up writing for "the trades." She talked so loud you could hear her over the dryers. One day she started making these typical anti-semitic remarks. It pissed me off, so I said, "Look, for someone who hates Jews so much, you seem to use Yiddish as your second language!" She told Indo she was very, very powerful in this town and could ruin my career. I ended up apologizing, but we never talked again. She eventually got fired from her job. I've run into her at various Hollywood events; she doesn't remember me. I watch her making insane facial expressions across the room. She still wears cap sleeves.

There is something hidden on everyone.

Judy* had a tiny rose directly above her left bun. I told her it was trashy and no man would ever want to be with her once he saw it, and she ran out of the room, crying. I would sit in the living room watching *Solid Gold*, hosted by Marilyn McCoo, and thumb through old copies of *Cosmopolitan*. Judy would pretend to fix a snack in the kitchen, but I knew that unless Gordy had been around, there was never anything in the place to eat, except maybe a jar of sweet pickle chips or a jar of mayonnaise with a thick, cracking yellow layer building around the sides. We all shared the one bedroom on nights they didn't make love, which were many—Gordy had gotten so fat.

Late at night he would melt butter in a frying pan, throw in a flour tortilla, packaged shredded cheddar cheese on top, fold it over and eat it hot out of the pan. Judy and I would take a bite. He'd make five or six more and wash them down with a carton of orange juice as he sat at the table with the gypsy tapestry and write his screenplay on yellow legal pads stained with grease and his dirty fingerprints.

Long after *The Tonight Show* ended, right into the dawn, he'd sit up snacking and writing as Judy and I would talk ourselves to sleep, she remorseful about the two kids she'd left back in Ohio. I never heard Gordy come into the bedroom and squeeze into Judy's twin bed. I couldn't understand how she managed to breathe with him pushing her up against the wall. One thing was certain: No matter how many times she or I got up in the middle of the night to use the bathroom, he never stirred, he'd sleep well into the hot West Hollywood afternoon.

Juan Montero* is off duty but going uptown; I'm going to Ninetieth and Central Park West; it's on his way, so he picks me up. The hair on his neck seems to crawl on his head and he's short and I like that. He's going on to Spanish Harlem, I assume, and the P.R. music is blaring in the front seat already as he counts his money and dodges buses.

Why do I like short men so much? Is it a sense of power and safety as I stand looking down on them? As if their dicks will be in proportion with their legs and arms —nothing overwhelming at all. Or maybe it's just a kind of raw sexiness.

Marshall was a lawyer from Missouri who drove a BMW and swore by Armorall to preserve the leather/vinyl interior. I dated him for a while in '77. He loved to expound on anything and loved L.A. Whenever we fucked, his breath smelled like tuna salad, and it was that, more than the actual act, that made me come.

There was a time when you spent the night with someone, and the next day they would send you a dozen long-stem roses with a sexy little note. Now people sent a bunch of balloons with cute cards saying such things as "Being with you last night was like having my own circus!"

I went to a black doctor for my abortion, at a women's clinic on Pico that looked safe. There was an old railroad car out front. I had gone there a few times before, for checkups; I got my first diaphragm there. My boyfriend was an aspiring actor and an expert on the New Wave/punk scene. He listened to Talking Heads' "Take Me to the River" over and over.

One night we went to the Ivar Theater to see some funky strippers who smoked cigarettes with their pussies. A lot of old men, à la Tom Waits, were grabbing the girls and whooping it up. It was one of the rare good times we had together. I treated him badly; he tried, but he always rubbed me the wrong way. When we got home that night, I felt close to him and very sexy, which I never did. I remember knowing immediately when we finished that I was pregnant—it was just one of those intuitive things.

I started getting nauseated in the morning and feeling premenstrual all the time. Finally, I went to the clinic on Pico for a test, which was positive. My boyfriend came with me the day I had the abortion. I made myself feel guilty about it—it was something so adult and so part of being a woman. He was Catholic and was very scared. He held my hand as they shot me up with Demerol. I fought the feeling of falling backward.

As I left afterward, I was pretty high, waving to

73

everyone to say what a good time I had had, thanking the black women in the waiting room. Friends came by to visit. I slept the rest of the day and went back to manicuring the next. I slept with my boyfriend only one more time.

She had one leg shaved, the other with hair.

They were both in the bathtub when I came home. "What the hell do you call this?" I screamed.

"I was shaving her other leg."

She just laughed, thinking I couldn't possibly be mad at her. I heaved my hairbrush at them; water splashed over the tub. They both dried off and tried to calm me down.

He left without another word. I told her I thought she was smarter than this.

"It was all for you," she said sadly.

"Well, that's just great. I feel *so* special."

After she left too, I threw all my sheets and towels into the washer and went to Alpha Beta to buy some chicken breasts for dinner.

I pick out from a tin assorted cookies that my aunt Zelda has made, piling them on an elaborate paper plate. With the cookies and a charcoal drawing of a Degas my uncle has done, I walk out to my car. Another California Christmas that I am convincing myself is not affecting me in any way.

As I drive up Sepulveda, in a world of my own, two giant fire trucks race before me, swinging down Wilshire. I throw on my brakes and the cookies slide onto the floor but do not come out of their careful wrapping. I extract a cookie and pop it into my mouth, trying to imagine how it will all be in twenty years, when my aunt and uncle will be ninety. I wonder if she'll make any cookies that Christmas, I think about the child I may or may not have, that Madonna will be regarded once again in the Christian sense, that friends will be scattered here and there, and I will know more about myself than I do today. But this is now, and I am still young and have some time to make certain decisions, which I continue to postpone.

Here on Sepulveda, past the military cemetery, a lot of self-control is exerted, fears are compacted down, recollections viewed swiftly, old loves romanticized, as only seasonal indulgence will allow. I long to become the best version of myself I can be. I look for perfection—the dusted table, the silken skin. I want fantasy to appear and never go away; I want all my papers in order and clutter down to a bare minimum. I want to have already happened, and yet I love it just the way it is.

The first weekend, they tapped electricity from the building with a big orange extension cord that ran right in front of my door. A couple of guys kept moving in motel furniture; the blond one had a bad perm and wore a Foot Locker striped referee's shirt, so I knew he sold tennis shoes. His taller, gangly friend had on jeans that kind of bagged at the ass and a heavy-metal T-shirt. They kept flicking cigarette ashes in the elevator.

One of the first nights they were there, I came home alone and fumbled with my keys, avoiding looking into the open door of their apartment. Two girls were there, and one looked at me. When I finally got my door opened, I heard her say, "Friendly neighbors you got here." I shut my door. The last people who moved in stayed thirteen days, and I was actually nice to them.

A few days later, I'm waiting in the elevator, and I hear their door open and someone running out; it's one of the girls, very young and shaky. "Hey, aren't you Sandra Bernhard? I've seen you on *Showtime* a hundred times. Do you like to swim? We could hang out sometimes."

"Well, I don't get out too much." I looked around.

"Well, how do you get a tan?"

I slipped into the elevator and waved.

A couple of days later, I'm typing away in my office, and again I hear the creepy sound of their apartment door opening, and then a knock on mine. I make myself very quiet and sneak out into the living room and peer through the peephole. She is there again, in a two-piece bathing suit, all wet, with mascara running under her eyes, waiting for me.

As it turns out, two sisters live there with the elder one's boyfriend or husband—essentially husband, because she has a baby. Both girls are not in school. The last time I'd seen one of them, she'd said, "Boy, you really don't get out much. I'm surprised you have any color."

I'd snapped, "I'm very busy," and rushed inside, feeling bad for her, but annoyed and irritable at the same time.

The thing that resonates in my mind more than anything is the soft Naugahyde bar that is the centerpiece of their living room. I can't help but think that it must be a kind of status symbol for them: coming home and fixing a cocktail, taking orders from behind the bar, opening a can of whiskey sour, pouring it over refrigerator ice in a paper cup from 7 Eleven, and belting it down. He plays with the baby as Janine or Debra or whatever the girls' names are makes hot dogs and cuts them up in tiny pieces for the baby. He takes out his wallet, unfolds his paycheck and waves it in front of them, admiring his overtime. He goes into the bathroom and squeezes a whitehead in the mirror and leaves his shirt hanging out as he changes to a Bud Light. He calls his buddy at the Foot Locker and invites him over for hot dogs and beers or a Mr & Mrs "T" cocktail of his choice. The girls don't care, as long as they have enough paper plates to go around.

They ask me if I could give them a ride to a party near the airport when I go out later. I tell them my boyfriend wouldn't like that.

I sometimes think: O.K., so maybe you won't leave a legacy to the world, like children you've lost touch with, who carry on your name, or a body of work collecting dust in someone's library. Isn't it really what you live every day, the interactions of people you love and respect—not who discusses you but the kind words that are spoken to your face? That is really all a legacy can provide—a hope for the living, a guide for their immortal beliefs. A remembrance can mean nothing to the one remembered; it can only remind the ones left behind how little they did while you were still alive.

I wake up out of a sound sleep and hear nothing. I leap out of bed to check on her. I turn on a sweet night light that throws off a pink glow and pull back her little knitted blanket. She is completely still. At first I don't want to believe it, but then, as I slowly pick her up, I sense that she is completely gone. I hold her up to my face, and there is nothing coming out of her. I sit down in an old rocking chair and try to gain my composure. "Jessie," I cry, "look at me. Come on, baby girl, you tiny little thing, open your eyes and look at me," but she doesn't.

I breathe into her mouth, remembering why I'd decided to call her Jessie. Suddenly, a tiny little rumble comes from within her. It turns into a loud cry. My knees buckle from under me and I start to cry with her. No one else hears me, and we talk for a long time, and Jessie seems to understand everything I tell her. I take her back to bed with me. My lover seems a little annoyed, and I don't try to explain what has just happened. Everyone sleeps but me.

Sally, Daniel and I were killing time before dinner at Salome Indian Restaurant on Lankershim.

As we drove past North Hollywood High, Sally's short dark hair blew back in her black Jeep. "Hey, didn't you go to school here?" I asked. She nodded yes. "Did you graduate?" She looked at herself in the rearview mirror and concentrated. "No, I shined it on and went to Hawaii." She turned into the alley before Lankershim.

The rest of the night had a kind of lonely warm breeze blowing through it, and if we talked, it was only a few words at a time.

Somewhere in oil country, her father kept an eye on her trust fund, and it made her lazy and unmotivated at times, but I was always around to remind her that she'd better not count on it and make her own money, just in case. It was the same part of me that cleaned compulsively, morning and night, grabbing the dustbuster to suck up the clumps of dust that seemed to grow each night and crawl out from under the couch.

In L.A., there are all these kids in their twenties who really mean well but have been exposed to dangerous levels of the dream world Hollywood is, and as a result they spend a lot of time studying their faces, having fat sucked out from under their eyes at twenty-eight, get involved with quick-money schemes, like the pyramid or most recently the "airplane," where a girl drummer who works during the day demonstrating food at Ralph's loses five hundred bucks because she joined in too late.

On the first night I light the Hanukkah candles and sing the prayer, Sally walks in and says really loud, "Hon, what sweater should I wear with this?" I stop, dumbfounded. "I can't believe you. I'm lighting the candles—don't you even care?" "Oh, I'm sorry. What do you think about this shirt with these pants? Be really honest."

Later, she asks me, "Honey, what was that song you were singing out in the kitchen before?" "It's the song blessing the Hanukkah candles." She laughs. "I didn't know what it was, but it was funny." "Well, fine. I'll laugh at something of yours on Christmas!" Sally walks away. "I don't care; just get me some good presents."

People ask me how I spend my nights. "Is it glamorous, Sandra?" And I tell them, Yes, in a way it really is. I begin with some freshening up in my bath, where I steam, scrub, buff, pluck, dig out ingrown hairs from a recent bikini wax. There in the bathroom, I stimulate follicles to grow and stare at tiny cracks and crevices, which need constant probing and scraping. Once a week I do an intense personal cleanup. Wednesdays and Saturdays, I shave my legs and underarms, usually in the afternoon, but on special occasions I'll get up early and do it in the morning. Today I'll be going to see my dermatologist for this mysterious dermatitis that keeps cropping up here and there. I think it may be a fungus.

People all over the country ask me my secret of success. I pause thoughtfully, and each time, without any doubts, I tell them it's my clean-as-you-go theory: Wherever I am, if I see dust collecting, you can be sure I'll dampen a piece of Kleenex or a paper towel and in one swift movement I'll be dust-free and thus clear to think all the important thoughts one requires to maintain a lifestyle such as this.

My most recent dinner at home featured a simple broiled veal chop with a lot of fresh garlic and tarragon, and my very special mashed potatoes, which I make from scratch, and steamed yellow squash with a squeeze of fresh lemon.

My most recent favorite evening at home included a crackling fire and listening to an old Heart album.

When I'm alone, I sleep with the TV on all night. I'll wake up at one-thirty and catch ten minutes of an old movie and then wake up again at four and think that the same movie is still on, that it somehow went from being a fifties horror movie to a western. Real early in the morning, I'll hear a sermon or religious discussion with a minister and some blond-haired older woman, and I'll jump up and quickly turn it off and then go to the bathroom, not bothering to flush it until I actually get up, a few hours later.

I'm lying in bed and something is scratching my leg and I pull back the covers and the little toenail on my right foot is totally pulled back. It's as if your little toe doesn't need the nail; the skin underneath is so tough and thick that the nail is merely there to protect you from the reality that your little toe is tough enough without it. On top of that, I have a miserable cold, so I go out to the kitchen and pour myself a cup of Nyquil. I go back to bed, to find I have a "leaky faucet," so I return to the kitchen, open the freezer and take out a package of vaginal suppositories. I insert one in front of the stove, rinse off the applicator in the sink and return the soggy box to the freezer, where it leans on a box of Stouffer's frozen macaroni and cheese and Tabatchnick's matzoh-ball soup in boil-in bags.

My feet look like a German Shepherd's back paws, really long and rabbit-like. They are perhaps the only part of my body that truly disturbs me, but I keep that under wraps because I believe when you say such things out loud, God punishes you and something really awful might happen to you. It's like if your nose isn't really that big but you suddenly get the urge to get it fixed, there is always the chance that it will turn out looking like a pig's snout, and maybe on some level you kind of deserve it. Needless to say, as far as my feet go, there is really nothing I can do to change them. So maybe they're a little too long and flat— so what if Norma Kamali said they looked like fish? I can move very efficiently with them, and when I wear the right heel, it gives them the arch they long to have.

My dad thinks I live in a world of my own. I am crying a little bit, driving home down Moorpark. I'm on my way home from someone else's family drama, which I enjoyed and participated in. Too many drinks, and suddenly you laugh in spite of the fact that your son is in the hospital. Cissy cries when her forty-year-old son goes out to toss his cookies and doesn't come back for an hour. He and his wife have split up. Maybe he got hit by a car. "Don't worry, Cissy," I tell her, as if I've known her for years, and I give her a hug. I drive Cissy around, looking for him, and he comes back while we're gone. Her circulation is bad and she's rubbing her legs all night, and then she comes in smoking a cigarette. I tell her it's bad for her circulation. She tells her son that he's crazy. "I've taken care of myself for forty years," he says. Somehow I've done all right." Cissy is laughing and hugs me for being sweet. A sister-in-law in a bugle-beaded dress quietly makes her presence known. A drunken brother-in-law strums a guitar and says he has his own pick in his wallet.

During the holidays, when a plane flies overhead in a smoky gray sky, I have a sense that somewhere in a house nearby a family has risen early to eat breakfast and light a fire. They talk quietly and play nice music. The son draws a picture and the mother reads a book about gardens and pours cream in her coffee. The father pauses to rub her shoulders before going out to work in the yard. I feel them over here in my world.

Marilyn died in Sally's arms on a Sunday in the back of a pickup on Tujunga.

I sat in the cab with Manny, our neighbor from across the street, sobbing and watching Sally kiss her face, that little tongue hanging out, her new teeth protruding like little chips of coral.

I'm walking down the street, calm and relaxed, not thinking about anything negative, when this dirty-looking white man in a baseball cap comes right up to my face and grabs me. Now, at first I'm stunned and frightened, but it takes me only a minute to get really angry. "Who the fuck do you think you are, you walking piece of shit?" I scream.

He pulls out a big ugly hunting knife and holds it to my throat and comes around behind me, giving me a half nelson and a cold blade. "Look, girlie, I ain't playin' around here. I come out to Hollyburg here to become a stuntman and a hero and I won't be leavin' till I do, and I just nominated you as my front-row ticket to fame and fortune, so now you and me are just gonna move right over to the Sports Connection and let some people get a gander at a girl and her knife."

"Well, this is real fun," I said back, in my own Kentucky Blue Ridge voice. "I reckon you could hurt me real bad with that there pig sticker, so let's mosey on over to the health club and you do your thing and we'll get to be really great friends!" This guy stinks like puke and booze. I'm scared out of my mind and keep thinking how I would like to beg and plead for my life, but something keeps telling me to humor him and not show any emotion.

We start attracting a small crowd now, which I

know is making him happy. People from a hair salon up above are looking down in horror and fascination. I smile up at them and wink.

"You like what you see? Just wait until I pierce the cheek—you all will get a big kick out of that." He's laughing now, all big smiles and stupid looks: I can feel him going through every emotion in the book, even though he's behind me.

As we cross the street, I feel his grip loosen and fall completely away. I look behind me and hear some women scream. He is lying face down with blood oozing out, and a couple of big West Hollywood cops in the distance are blowing smoke away from their rifles. My hero has just received his Academy Award.

In the spring, when you move the clock forward at 2 A.M. on a Saturday night, that feeling of despair sets in. Everything is out of your hands again; you feel like a snail without a shell. I get on the phone and make small talk with just about anyone who'll listen. And all that I'm really looking for is someone who will tell me that the overwhelming beauty of spring will pass; the falseness of nature, which pricks my instincts, will blossom fully, and once again leaves will wither and lose their color and I will feel safe. In the fall, nothing ever seems as sad as a bud on a tree, the smell of night-blooming jasmine or a row of peas pushing themselves up through the earth.

When summer comes and the dark shades of winter retract deep into the quieter parts of the mind, the body takes over and relaxes into the sand and heat and careless sensuality that a little bit of coconut oil seems to bring out in the best of us. In California, the only true season is the one of endless summer, and even the outsiders like me (who but for the grace of God could just as well have been staring out over a bleak, endless Russia) seem to get caught up in it.

I watch casually the new crop of beautiful young boys, each more confident than the next, muscular and dumb, sand caught deep in their ears, and a blond hair that no other sunlight in the world creates. It's a kind of symmetry and excitement that makes me buy stupid outfits all in white. You notice the surf trunks that ride low on their asses, exposing the very top of a sweet white crack, all young and soft; teeth that sun bounces off; and a stripe of zinc oxide across the cutest noses and the fullest lips. I check them out, lonely faggots check them out, they check each other out, lost in the unspoken vows of the waves and the blue sky. I watch them in a deeply envious state—a world of the whitest light, and slow, lush obsessions.

Even though she'd been on a painfully dull diet for a year
and a half and had lost a hundred and fifty pounds, there
was something about her that hadn't changed. It was the
way she carried herself, the lumbering stilted movement,
the rush of wind left behind, the greasy sweaty look of her
forehead and nose, which just never seemed to get resolved.

No matter how she dressed herself up, she remained
the imposing circus figure she had been her entire life, and
it perpetuated all the insanity that surrounded her. She
always seemed to be getting over bronchitis, and recently
she'd taken to wearing enameled earrings, which accen-
tuated the loose skin around her neck when she coughed.

She owed me a thousand dollars, which I loaned her to
buy a car. It came to the point where I just didn't care
anymore, as long as I didn't have to endure her long stories
of suffering, of disasters near and missed. I looked at it as
an investment in the distance one needed to keep from her
in order to avoid getting sucked into her personal black
hole.

She lived in a kind of triplex house up in Hollywood Hills, with the lowest ceiling I'd ever experienced.
Her five cats all looked and acted exactly like her; they were
the focus of her love and affections. They slept with her
and watched her eat with the same greed with which she
watched everyone else.

On a recent trip to New York, I found myself with some time on my hands, and I realized how lonely I was. Friends sensed it and urged me to try and meet a nice guy, just for an evening out. I felt resistant. All those Wall Street types just turned me off; younger men were becoming a bore.

A really close girlfriend called me up one day and said, "Honey, what are you doing tonight? I think I've got someone you're going to like a lot. I don't want to tell you too much, but does Isaac Bashevis Singer ring a bell?"

"Cheryl, you're kidding me! He's every girl's dream! I would kill to go out with Isaac. I've had a thing for him ever since he autographed my copy of *The Magician of Lublin*. He's fabulous, and I really picked up on a great vibe from him. Is this for real, because if it is, I've got to start pulling it together. I look like hell!"

"Yes, baby, it's definitely for real. He loves your work and wants to take you to Memphis for dinner."

"Oh, I think I'd rather stay in town—only kidding. Gosh, he sounds very cool."

"He is, darling, and he'll be by in a car at nine-thirty for drinks. I'll call you tomorrow. Oh, by the way, just be yourself. Love you!"

He picked me up a half hour late and apologized profusely; he'd had an overseas call and couldn't get off. He hated what I was wearing and rushed me over to

Comme Des Garçons to buy me a man-tailored suit. He said he liked his women butch. Who was I to argue? Dinner was incredible. He kept whispering sexy things in Yiddish in my ear, running his hand across my thigh, barking orders to the waiters to bring more Cristal and to make it snappy, he didn't have time to waste, couldn't they see he was with a beautiful woman! He kept getting up and going to the bathroom. "Isaac honey, I think you'd better wipe off your nose." He laughed and kissed me hard, dribbling champagne into my throat.

We left and went dancing at Palladium, where every gorgeous woman in the place was all over him like cheap perfume, but he laughed it off and swung me around the dance floor like Sterling St. Jacques. He introduced me to some model he'd gone out with and kept pushing for a three-way, but I started getting jealous at that point and told him I wanted to go home. He finally figured it out that I wanted to be alone with him and that he was close to blowing it, so he grabbed my hand and we ran up those stairs into the limo, and it all started right then and there.

By the time we got back to his place, a penthouse at Trump Tower, he slapped on a pair of handcuffs and told me to put on this black teddy he'd bought for me. He smacked me across the face and screamed something in Russian, a throwback to his childhood. He cried and told me he was tired of playing the intellectual, that he really wanted to experience life now. I held him in my arms until the sun came up. After finding the key to the handcuffs, I kissed him gently on the cheek and left.

He called me for weeks on end, but I told my maid to pretend I was out on the Coast. He was just too needy, and I felt I couldn't be there for him. It broke my heart when the necklace from Cartier arrived, with a note reading: "In all my years of magic, never have I been as bewitched. Keep the necklace forever. Say nothing and I will know how much you care. Such a *shayner maydl*. With love and loneliness, Isaac." I wept in the bathtub. Cheryl told me I was insane, but I knew I would destroy him eventually, so I went back to my quiet days and empty New York nights.

In an office building, a girl from Queens with long purple nails and a copy of the zipper dress by Azzedine Alaia is clicking down the hallway. Only her high heels give her away as she rushes toward the ladies' room to see if she leaked through. She makes it in the nick of time, droplets of blood just starting to work their way down her tampon string. She smells a little metallic mixed with the Poison her boyfriend gave her for her birthday, just three weeks before. She excitedly anticipates the office Christmas party —chatting with the girls—the secretaries, the office manager—flirting with guys in suits that are just a little bit off: the material is wrong or the collar on the shirt too long; you can't really pinpoint it when he's in motion, but when he stops for coffee, or to drop off a memo, and you have that extra second to take it in, you see right away that this guy is barely making it.

Only the secretaries stay efficient at Christmas. They know too well how quickly it goes by and that the more relaxed you get, the harder it is to face the coldest months ahead, which are not adorned with tinsel and tiny glistening lights or romantic notions about anything. A girl cannot afford to get her hopes too high in this season. You've got to keep in mind you're never going to be Sheila E. or Grace Jones. Dreams are reserved for those who can boldly strike out on *Dance Fever* or *Puttin' on the Hits,* or who have the guts to go out to L.A. These girls see it come and go; they brush elbows with coffee achievers, with coke fiends who slip them an envelope with a twenty or a fifty. They can't let on that it means anything, even to themselves. It's a short walk down into the subway, but it's a long ride, a lonely, hurtful ride back home through so many tunnels, with many others left behind as worthless, bearing scars from pimples squeezed too soon, or tattoos etched on the tops of fingers. There is this sad, listless look on some black woman's face as she tries to hold on to her bags, her Soul Train products, and fish something out of her purse, with all of fifty dollars in it, some coupons, a lipstick by Flori Roberts, and a set of keys to the place she cleans on Central Park West.

No, these people will not be meeting anyone for tea at the Mayfair Regent after shopping on Madison, or catching *Wild Honey* with Ian McKellen (even though they think it will be some stupid little clichéd English farce) and then out for a late dinner at The Canal Bar.

This world does not, will never exist for these people who dare to creep into Manhattan every day to help push the machine along and hope for the chance to say they ran into Isabella Rossellini: "There she is over there, that chick from the movie, you know, *Blue Velvets,* the one who walks around all fucked up and naked—yeah, that one!"

There was Christmas, another hand-it-over, live-it-up, pay-in-February holiday season, meant to be enjoyed only by the manipulative, or those with trust funds.

I am watching it from a friend of a friend's apartment in the Village, getting into the roommate of the friend of a friend's bed with nasty grit on my feet. I rub them together and pull some weird blanket around me, because I cannot bear to be out on those cold sad lonely streets another minute. At least, in California, everyone looks the same—strangely comfortable, healthy, detached. Someone else is watching too, and when I look up to smile, she pulls down her blinds.

"Passionate love and a little money, that's all I want!"

The checkout clerk at Mrs. Gooch's was telling me how she felt about her long days behind the cash register, and I really sympathized. I was careful to hide my fifties in my wallet, they looked so obscene. I couldn't bear to hurt her anymore.

When I got home, I opened the package of Brie cheese I had bought for a snack, and it smelled horrible, almost like crap, but I put some on a Carr's water cracker and ate it anyway. It tasted sour and watery, and the smell stayed on my fingers as I drove back to return it. I whispered to the same lady that it was rotten. She looked sad. "Poor baby, go back and get something else." The new cheese was about twenty-seven cents more, but she told me just to go ahead; it was all right. The bad cheese was left sitting on a ledge next to her cash register.

My parents' divorce is final this year and my dad won't even look at my mom. I pull down the menorah and set it on a piece of aluminum foil on the counter. There are drops of colored wax from the past three Hanukkahs on it. There are at least three different ways to spell Chanukah; now you've seen two of them.

"There is nothing I could possibly want or need after masturbating. Everything seems to have lost its luster," said Judy at her party celebrating the new Beaujolais. There are times in L.A. or New York when I am so lonely that I'll pretend to find something significant even in honoring a glass of red wine.

Judy was older or looking that way. I really loved her at one time. I'd spend hours with her alone or with her and her boyfriends, who came and went. I liked her Xerox art, even though it was mainly of her face or costume jewelry or a tube of toothpaste and toothbrushes thoughtfully arranged. Her poetry was not inspired, and yet I was involved for a while in a reading of it. Her poems were about hopes of womanhood and deep Jewish late-thirties guilt. Judy always tried to make events out of everything.

She married a carpenter who looked like Louise Nevelson and got rich by building new bathrooms in extravagant people's homes. I drank more Freixenet champagne with them than I care to remember.

Judy wanted to recreate the great salons of Paris in the '20s, where everyone contributed—or at least so we are led to believe—insightful, brilliant moments in history, in self-imposed exile from their homes in America, while longing to return. This is how Judy imagined us all.

She wrote songs with our friend Merrill,* whom she had known since college. She still talked about it like it was yesterday, as if they were naive and fresh and discovering life for the first time. There's nothing more unappealing than a woman over thirty pretending to be innocent.

Merrill would perform along with her boyfriend Jimmy* at the Bla Bla Café in Studio City. There was always an air of excitement, as if it was all ready to happen. I'd sit with my arm around Judy, listening to the saddest of their songs. Merrill would introduce Judy, and she'd stand up and take a dramatic bow. She was always arriving late, as if it was expected from such an important talent.

Our friendship fell apart when good things started to happen for me. She sent a horrible letter to me in New York, telling me how I had fallen right into being a star, "basking in the glory of the kleig lights." It was jam-packed with original phrases such as that. I've lost a few friends along the way, but it was never that transparent, always more subtle, and usually I could sense the anger before it manifested itself.

THE TINT INSTITUTE

I went to meet my friend Bev at The Ginger Man in Beverly Hills after I performed one night, and when I walked in, she was talking to this blond in a low-cut sweater, with big tits. Bev is a psychologist from San Diego and manages to find something interesting in just about everyone she meets. I walked over in my big tweed coat I got in Philadelphia.

Her name is Suzzane Tint; she was a theater sophomore at USC. She was guzzling a Greyhound and laughing loudly. She knew who I was and was being very seductive in that sophomoric kind of way, making innuendos, etc. I noticed a large mole stuck in her cleavage. Bev liked her sweater, and that's how the whole thing started. It made me wish Bev had better taste. By the time Suzzane asked for my number, Bev had moved on to someone else, and I had to track her down to get out of there as quickly as possible.

A few weeks went by. I hadn't thought too much about Suzzane, when she called and invited me over for dinner at her apartment off campus. I was a little nervous driving down to that part of town. When I got there, I buzzed her for at least five minutes. I gave it one more long buzz, and her voice, a little hazier than I had remembered, crackled through the intercom. Mumbling something indiscernible, she let me in. I walked up a flight of stairs and knocked on her door. When she opened it she was wearing a rubber neck collar and her eyes were red and swollen. She had on a thin blue terry-cloth bathrobe and was on the phone. "I'm O.K.," she kept crying. She covered the mouthpiece and told me she had been in an accident on the freeway and had just been released from the hospital. She moved her hand. "Mom, my friend Sandra is here. Will you tell my mom I'm all right?" She handed me the phone. "Hello, Mrs. Tint. Yes, she seems to be all right. Yes, I'll make sure she's all right. Here's Suzzane. Bye now. No problem."

I started to walk around the apartment. It was run down and shag-carpeted. Filthy. It hadn't been vacuumed in months; there were sticky glasses on the coffee table and a funky turntable rotating with no record. I eased into the kitchen and looked carefully into the sink. There was a pile of pans, plates and glasses that had been there, it seemed, for at least two weeks. An amazing array of mold cultures grew in the glasses, small clusters of black and longer gooey green strips; I quickly looked the other way as Suzzane came in.

"I'm so sorry the place is such a mess. I can't believe this happened today. There was no way for me to reach you. I still want to make you dinner. I bought everything." I kind of looked at her in amazement; she seemed like some weird animal, with that collar on. She kept telling me she

100

had to stay up all night in case she had a concussion. I guess she expected me to volunteer. I never did.

She called her little friend from upstairs, a gay Mexican kid from the theater department, named Tommy. He seemed concerned and started to explain Suzzane to me, how messy she is, crazy but brilliant. He told her to lie down while he did the dishes.

He talked to me about USC and how great the theater department was. Suzzane finally came in and started peeling potatoes. "Tommy, the guy smashed right into me. What am I going to tell my father?"

"Honey, it's not your fault, don't worry. I'll stay with you tonight and make sure you're all right." He finished the dishes, which took a good forty-five minutes. I admired him for his loyalty. He gushed over me for a minute and left, giving Suzzane a wink.

It was awkward as she prepared dinner, which turned out to be Oscar Meyer wieners cut lengthwise, stuffed with mashed potatoes, a piece of American cheese laid over it, and put under the broiler until it bubbled.

When I left that night, I got the feeling I wouldn't be seeing her again. But the next thing I knew, I was beginning to discover things about her I never wanted to know. Her father was a Wall Street mogul now working for a home-seed company; her mother remained in New York, playing socialite, gold digging here and there as the alimony ran out; Suzzane had worms off and on and had to carry her stool samples in a plastic specimen cup to the doctor; she used to have little bits of toilet paper stuck to her crotch, which she never noticed; and her fingernails were long and had chipped Misty Mocha polish that she would keep painting over.

I spent an entire summer with her in New York while she went to summer school at NYU. After she told her mother about us, I couldn't stay at her condo. I was an opening act at a club for a hundred bucks a night and spent most of it on hotels. I had an incessant case of diarrhea and was the skinniest I'd ever been. It was hot and muggy and sickening there.

She told me endless stories about the Manhattan elite and how her mother got snubbed by all the wives of investors. Her mother worked for Sotheby's and went out with gross balding men who got drunk and tried to fuck her. Suzzane, her sister and her mother all went to Club Med one time and got laid; that was apparently a very significant bond between the three of them. I sat in like it was the kind of seminar where you know you won't get your money's worth, but you're stuck.

After the long summer, I drove across country with Suzzane. The day before we left, she went in for uterine cryosurgery. Her mother packed us egg-salad sandwiches and chocolate-chip cookies and left a note telling her "two girls" to please be safe. During the whole drive across country from one Big Mac to the next, Suzzane got stinkier and stinkier, trapped all day in her Toyota Celica. She wore yellow shorts. Liquid oozed out onto a maxipad she changed every two days.

Somewhere in New Mexico, she took me to a country-and-western bar, her favorite movie being *Urban Cowboy*. I was dancing really close, kind of grinding, with some giant truckdriver, when she came running over and tried to break us up. If I hadn't run after, she would have left me there. Back at the motel, we had a scene where I cried and went to sleep in the closet. She tried to pick me up and put me back in bed—she was a big girl.

The last I heard about her, she had opened in a small theater in L.A. She'd co-written a feminist play called *Flesh and Sapphires.*

"Skinny like me," in 1977 she decided to go underground and live incognito among the thin.

Cher does this commercial for the Holiday Health Spas. With her super bright teeth and amazing breasts photographed at perfect angles, she could convince, with that detached angry voice, anyone to get up off the couch and lay out the eighteen bucks a month it costs to join; it's membership by intimidation.

Recently I had an "incident" at the club out on Victory, deep in the Valley. I've been a member since 1975;

I joined on one of those deals where after the first year you become a life member at thirty-five dollars a year. Somehow it's the one thing that stayed constant through all my years in L.A.

One evening, I went to work out with a friend of mine. She had forgotten her driver's license. They have all these rules, like you have to bring your membership card and your driver's license and you can't wear sleeveless T-shirts and you have to bring a lock for your locker but you can't leave it on overnight or else they'll cut it off.

We signed in and they asked for my friend's license and I said, "Look, we just want to work out real quick and get in and out. My friend here is a new member, as you can see by her card, and she didn't remember the license thing—you guys know me here." The girl named Barbie came out of an office; I knew by her name I was in trouble. She wore a lot of makeup and high heels, and had a very professional attitude. She tersely explained that under no circumstances would we be allowed in without the driver's license. She got more incensed as we persisted. I wanted to fuck with Barbie a little. "This is insane," I said. I said, "Come on, big deal. Bend the rules a little, Barb! Live life on the edge!" At this point she grabbed my card and license and ran into an office. I ran right in after her. "Look here, Barbie, this is bullshit and I'm going to kick your ass if you don't give me back my card!"

"I already have all your information, and I'll call the police if you don't get out of here." "Go right ahead. What are you going to tell them, you stupid bureaucratic cunt!" I was ranting and raving, and Barbie grabbed my wrist as I took back my card and license, my girlfriend joining in. It was a terrible scene.

So a year and a half goes by. I continue to work out at the spa, and I realize I have not received my new card in the mail. I call and apparently Barbie has canceled my membership due to the aforementioned "incident," which is how they keep referring to it. I become hysterical—it's as if the last vestiges of my recent past have been taken away. I interpret it as a bad omen and try to figure out a scheme to make it right. It is that feeling you have when you make a bad left-turn into an oncoming car and later replay the scene over and over, saying to yourself, "If I had only stopped at the 7 Eleven, none of this would have ever happened." I wake up in cold sweats, I can't concentrate on my work. I begin breaking out with strange patches of dermatitis. If only I could somehow rectify the situation and be taken back as a lifetime member.

I kept sneaking in in spite of the cancellation. They caught me one day as Kristy McNichol was signing in. Their anger and contempt was so great that I felt like a victim of a fascist coup. For once in my life, I knew I had to remain calm and exhibit total restraint. I talked to Mike, one of the managers, who then connected me with Kim, who was pretty nice and listened to my story. She would have to take it in front of the board for review. A decision was reached the next day, and Kim was pleased to announce that I had been reinstated. I should go to the club and see Mike, who would explain the "rules" to me. I went and bit my tongue as he told me to be sure to bring my driver's license every time I signed in. He finally admitted that Barbie no longer worked for the company and that she had indeed been "pretty intense." "Yes," I said. "I think she was having a bad day."

I walked out with my temporary membership card.

My "gold card" would be put in the mail. I thanked the Lord for the newfound acceptance I had been granted.

He nailed me the minute I walked through the doors of the Federated—flaky skin on his face and hands, dandruff, and breath that greeted me before the doors had closed. "Hi, can I help you?" he asked in unctuous tones.

"Yes; I'm looking for a car stereo, something in the three-hundred-dollar range."

"Great. Come right this way. Your name?"

"Sandra."

"Hi, Sandra, I'm Doug."

"Hi. Show me something in a knob control. This is a gift for a friend. She doesn't like digital controls. You guys have anything these days like that?"

"Oh, yes, Sandra. In that case, let me show you something right over here, by Pioneer. It's an analog model, very good quality. Now listen to it with the booster; you see, it needs that extra power to drive those speakers. Now, what kind of a car do you have?"

I settled in for a long haul. He kept leaning into me, as if demonstrating his flaky scalp and dirty bottom teeth. "Well, it's not my car. It's my friend's car. I borrowed it for the day and had to make up this story that I'd get it washed for her, so I've only got a few hours to pull this all together. It's an eighty-five Mustang convertible."

"Well, Sandra, you're a very good friend. Let's go out and look at it to figure how many speakers we'll need and how it should sound, O.K.? I can tell you're a lady of very good taste."

I realized my sunglasses, hooked on my T-shirt, were pulling it down to a point where he might be able to see my breasts, so I put them on as we walked out to the car. By the look on his face, I got the feeling that he thought we were going out on a date.

He opened the door and asked me to get in on the passenger side so we could listen together. It seemed to take him fifteen minutes to listen to this shitty factory stereo. He leaned over me brushing against my leg as he rolled up the window.

I thought he had finished, so I got out and locked the doors. He said, "Oh, Sandra, would you mind opening the door again. I want to look at the speakers in the back-seat." I stood there feeling greasy, wanting to run home and brush my teeth and cut my toenails—anything to nullify the exposure to his rotten breath. He once again demonstrated the way it could be set up. Finally, we went back in to decide on the speakers. "Well, Sandra, these are very nice, but if you like those, you should listen to these Infinitys. (Seemed I *had* been listening to infinity.)

"No, Doug, I think I like these Alpines better, so I'll take those and the Pioneer tape deck." By then I had the resignation of someone who had just been denied parole.

He started to write up my sale while trying to talk me into a five-year warranty for forty dollars, but I politely refused, staring at his dry hands. "O.K. Thanks a lot, Doug. I'll just carry it out myself." I picked up the two hateful boxes and started to follow him up front. He stopped halfway.

"Sandra, look, if you happen to find yourself at our other seminar—I mean, store—this afternoon, having the stereo installed by Jim . . ." I knew it; finally, everything came together. This guy was a seminar freak, and from each one had gathered up more and more confidence. "Anyway, I'll look for you and take you across the street and we can have a nice talk and some drinks."

"Oh, that's very nice, if I'm there. Definitely. Look for me, O.K.?"

"Well, Sandra, even if you're not there, I'd like to take you out anyway. If I can have your number and call sometime, I'd really like that." (Oh, you would, would you? Fuck off before I nail your three-inch dick to the wall of a Pep Boys. Get my drift, you stinky creep?)

"Well, no, I can't do that, Doug. I'm seeing somebody, and it just wouldn't work out, but thanks anyway."

"Well, Sandra, I really enjoyed meeting you. Maybe we'll see each other again sometime." (Not even in your dreams, Dickweed.)

I, as calmly as I could, walked up to the front desk. He led me to the "right" side, where a girl with a wandering eye and a strange accent rang me up.

I ran out the door to my car and noticed Doug leaning on another car, smoking a cigarette. He started walking toward me. "You look so familiar. What do you do, Sandra?"

"I'm a writer, Doug."

"Would I have read anything by you?"

"I don't think so, but keep your eye out; maybe something soon."

I practically caught his nose in my door as I turned on the engine with a vengeance. He kept talking through the closed window, taking on a carnival look, his lips flapping in exaggerated movements. "I'll look for you—a book or something."

"O.K., Doug."

In New York this wouldn't be late, but it's L.A.

I'm not tired, and I can't imagine when I ever will be. I want to go for a walk, but I'm afraid I'll run into a serial killer at the 7 Eleven, having a cup of coffee. Unless I want to get dressed and put gas in my car, I'd better just dream about what's waiting for me out there.

All my friends are away. There's no one to call. If it were 1972, we would all be living in Laurel Canyon, writing songs about just a little green or my old man, rapping about Jim Morrison and last time we saw him in leather, fucked up and beautiful.

It is 1987, and unless I force it, nothing spontaneous will occur on this moist May night. I long for it, desire it, and I close my eyes, slipping into that hesitating dream state, traveling in and out of memories of all we've been forced to leave behind.

The blonde in a black jumpsuit cut off at the ankles is singing Sade, standing uneasily off center to the mike as the band jams in a mellow kind of way. She tries to look detached. I keep watching her, and it's as if she could break down and cry at the toss of a bouquet or at the couple's "very first dance," to something like "Close to You." She sings with her eyes closed, occasionally pushing back her hair or taking a sip of water.

The mood suddenly changes as the bandleader urges everyone down to the floor to do the hora. Everyone in the place is up—the fat women with their shrunken husbands, looking pleased with themselves; an aunt just in from Century Village in Florida ("David Letterman's father lived there for a while; I met him when I was going door to door for a UJA pledge, but I think he's moved away"); teenage girls with braces, fashionable haircuts and velvet dresses, coaxed by their girlfriends, who are eyeing gangly boys. Couples married for two and a half years stay seated, looking as if they regret the day they met, and the bride and groom, with a false sense of hysteria, are lifted in the air on gold chairs, playing a king and queen ruling uncomfortably and serenely.

All during the hora, the singer stands awkwardly, shifting her weight from foot to foot, looking mainly down at the floor or at her stilettos, which desperately need new heels, wondering why she wore them to begin with, starting to hate her whole outfit, wishing she were back in Honolulu, singing at the Hyatt Lounge.

The mood changes once again as the fathers make toasts. "May Shelly and David get to know the love my wife and I have experienced. May their love be a sweet one that blossoms with the years, and if I can help out in any way, don't hesitate to ask, but please, nothing over fifty thousand, O.K? Ha ha."

"And now something for the kids." The singer is back up on her feet, and she and the band launch into a fifties medley. Teenage boys are dancing with their mothers, who won't let go.

Such beautiful curves, I was thinking, all the marvelous melodies in the world. Smooth, elliptical stones broken off jagged cliffs overlooking the sea, foamy waves that have beaten them into quiet coves, where we finger them while carrying on soft distant conversations.

"You could surf; you shouldn't knock it till you try it." He pretended he didn't know who I was.

"You see, the problem is that I'm really a shitty swimmer, and I panic very easily."

He kept looking ahead at the ocean, as if he knew something I didn't. "Well, that's O.K. A lot of guys are scared. You could learn real fast; I could show you how."

I kept thinking seriously about it, as if I had to satisfy this total stranger, knowing damn well I had a pact with God that I would never venture too far out into the sea, or fly in private planes, or skydive, or do anything stupid like that, but I was in the mood to tempt fate and go against the ground rules, my own bottom line, just because this boy was so cute and reassured me that nothing could possibly happen.

What he didn't understand was that just getting wet above my waist in that cold dirty green ocean made me sick —Mexicans shit in the water here—but he grabbed me by the hand, this Hank or Dave or Mike. "You like Christmas in L.A.? I'm right here surfin' every Christmas morning since I was seven, except the one year my old man dragged us all to New York to have a real winter Christmas and I just sat in the hotel room and drew pictures of the waves. Maybe I'll go back there sometime with you, or something."

What a great thing to say, I thought to myself. How can I possibly let this guy down? I took his hand and carried the borrowed board in the other as we did that amazing "surfer run" down to the water, and without stopping, without hesitation, I dove in with him, threw the board underneath me and jumped on it like I'd done it a thousand times before, as if I were some beautiful Gentile goddess who had returned to the water. We paddled out together, all thoughts of catastrophes behind me, of sucking in seawater or cramping or just getting swept away. He was right there next to me, a perfect white scar on his shoulder, a

112

chipped tooth, a totally honest look in his eyes. He got close enough to kiss me and did. It was so crazy and Waspy, so much fun, and we stayed out there for a while and I tried to stand up a couple of times and fell over, and he kept yelling, "It's cool, you got it, it's totally cool."

I was shopping at Bullock's and came upon this outfit by Adrienne Vittadini, which brought up all kinds of painful memories and intense emotions. It had a little stand-up collar and three rows of gold buttons, and looked like an outfit Jackie Kennedy would have worn. When I tried it on I started to cry. I closed my eyes and saw John John running around JFK's office, a game of touch football with Ethel standing in the background, Lee Harvey Oswald bent over, clutching his stomach, a fedora-clad Jack Ruby holding a gun.

I must have passed out, because the next thing I knew, the salesgirl was hanging up the dress and offering me a glass of water. I'll never forgive Adrienne Vittadini for what she did to me.

the funkiness of new york is overwhelming.
in my room, by the door, it smells like a rat got stuck in
the wall and died and is decaying there.
on the street, the color of people's skin is sallow, gray
and very scary.
i am in the midst of the alienation and loneliness that only
new york can create.
on the subway, in a cab, walking in a daze on university
place, I have an underlying sense of memory, time and
sadness at where i've been and who i am.
this city isn't romantic anymore.
i fell in love here. there was excitement and success.
from hotel windows it sparkles.
from spanish harlem windows it lies smudged with
indelible creases and marks of time lost, divided and
rediscovered.
for the past ten visits it doesn't remind me of you anymore.
and for that i am very happy.

It was all New Yorkese, that mumbling, paranoid kind of thing they all get into: "It's like this, you must understand, this can never be, no one can know these things, it's a very, very private matter, and if you work with us, we've got to have this kind of trust, and then we don't have to discuss it any further."

These cryptic conversations go back and forth about and around you until you start agreeing with them about everything—the government, films, food and so on. After a while, I was talking about things I'd never seen or heard of and was convincing even myself that I had.

I wore a gray wool skirt and a sleeveless embroidered blouse from Mexico the day he asked me back for my second audition. I waited in the lobby of the Chateau Marmont for an hour and a half, just sitting in one position and focusing on what I wanted to do for them that day. Someone came out to tell me Marty wasn't feeling well, his asthma was acting up, and could I come back tomorrow. I left feeling exhausted but content with tomorrow's prospect. The next day I put on the same outfit and went back. Both he and Bobby apologized for the rescheduling. During the entire audition process, I never let them see anything except raw emotion and a kind of mock anger that I relied heavily on in those days. After a month they had flown me first class to New York and put me up at the Mayflower, where I'd bump into Robert Duvall and Joe Pesce and all those tough guys who seem not to really like women.

I met Jerry Lewis on a Wednesday. He was everything I expected and more. For the first time I was afraid. I read with him and they told me later he thought I was very convincing and was afraid of me too. I waited around for a couple or more days. Marty had me over for dinner and played me Joan Jett and Warren Zevon. We sat looking out at the New York skyline toward the East River. I was wearing baggy jeans and a pink cable-knit sweater from The Gap. I felt the strain of my clothes all around me, as if I had just arrived from some hick town. I felt passionate, sexy in a way I'd never felt. All this precious power surrounded me: assistants setting four video machines to record things off the TV for the "archives"; pictures of him and Isabella Rossellini, who was forever on her way to Italy. I sat on the edge of Marty's bed, with all the asthma medication, pitchers of ice water, an oxygen tank and posters of exotic films I'd never seen, with James Mason and Lee Van Cleef.

On that Friday, Cis, the casting director, called me up to let me know I had got it. I sat there in Room 310 with my friend Belle Zee and had this kind of strange letdown feeling. I never allowed anyone to know about it, but I felt empty and alone. I called everyone who mattered, but I never felt connected to any of it.

I am a casual participant in a game that everyone swears means nothing at all. And I live in the Valley. I could kill Moon Zappa for misrepresenting us out here; it's really nothing like that. It's a quick hop over Laurel Canyon, an escape from the ugliness of West Hollywood and the dangers of Beverly Hills. It's a place where you can formulate your own point of view, because it isn't demanding, or jam-packed with hustlers and actresses looking for sugar daddies.

People are just a little bit "geeky," but they mind their own business in great little Spanish houses off Moorpark. When I drive through Studio City late at night, I get old familiar safe feelings, and I pull into my garage without looking over my shoulder. I watch from my bedroom window as cars and trucks with good values head west on the Ventura Freeway, crisscrossing the night, spewing out their own particular hopes and disappointments practically on my doorstep as they glide by.

Even in my sleep I hear these conversations going on between drunk drivers and the highway patrol, who, in low tones, tell them to "get off the freeway, take the next off ramp, no, don't stop, get off at Coldwater, slow down, get off now, did you hear me, now!" Sometimes I wake up crying, thinking I've done something really bad and I'm going to get arrested. I lie there terrified to get up and go to the bathroom or get a drink of water.

Here in the Valley, in North Hollywood, I have uncomplicated feelings, and the further north I drive, the less complicated they become. It's mile after mile of people who don't have a bone to pick, who aren't waiting to sell a script or star in a TV series. We live in buildings with names like the Presidential Terrace, which have spacious living rooms and dishwashers. I know in my heart I must move on to bigger and better things, but I just can't seem to let go of the innocence and simplicity. With Gelson's to the left of me and Mrs. Gooch's to the right, my needs are completely met. Why would I want to venture away? Farther out, on Victory, where it starts to get a little on the white-trash side, I work out at the Holiday spa, the one Cher advertises for in one of her big, scary hairdos.

Joan Jett is from the Valley. I think all the Runaways, the forerunners of all the girl groups of the eighties, are. These girls tore up the Valley, really lived it their way, in shag haircuts and blue eye shadow and platform tennis shoes, at underage bars like the Sugar Shack when it was really cool to be "bisexual" and get nasty on Quaaludes. The Valley is the most romantic part of L.A. Everyone looks ready to fall in love—the surf boys on skateboards, adorable girls in post-Madonna outfits, some on Honda Elites, with perfectly blown hair, renting videos on the curve and gossiping at Du Par's over a short stack of buttermilk pancakes and a diet Coke.

The Valley stretches on for a thousand miles in each direction. You can leave the country on Ventura Boulevard. I've driven for fourteen hours and never reached the end. Of course, all roads lead eventually to the beach, where even the most staunch Valleyites end up at one time or another. You always know—even in June, when the beach is socked in fog—that the Valley will be sunny, and if you're above Ventura, just south of the hills, you will see the panorama that seduces me to stay. From convenience of the Burbank Airport, past Val Surf, as far as the eye can see past Encino, to the banks of smoggy mountains, to the Fatburger next to Tower Records, I am in awe, deeply committed and content. Far away from midwestern morals and East Coast sophistication, without the guilt or remorse of old family money, I am one of the anonymous.

"Celebrity Party, starring Sandra Bernhard, party hearty, be a party animal!"

I went home to visit my father and his girlfriend, Bonnie. They're living in a patio home out in Scottsdale (a development called Santa Fe), painted in that desert coral. Inside, the living room is adorned with two pillars made from poured cement, an aqua leather chair and footstool, a glass coffee table with a plexiglass candy dish that says "Have a Nosh with Jerry and Bonnie."

In the corner is the kind of Egyptian-shaped lamp that you turn on by merely touching the stand: sometimes, when the phone rings, the vibrations turn it on or make it brighter. I am sitting on the couch watching a Whitesnake video, Tawny Kitane seducing David Coverdale, and my dad is next to me as I explain the MTV concept.

They're throwing me a party, and they've sent out these fliers: "Celebrity Party, starring Sandra Bernhard!"

My grandmother called last week to tell me that she and Bonnie were also going to surprise my dad with a cake for his sixty-fifth birthday, which was in a couple of weeks, and told me to wear a dress. "You have a dress, don't you, honey? Jeans are fine in the day, but not for a party."

I paused, "Yes, Grandma, I think I have a dress."

"Are you dating any boys, honey?"

"Yes, Grandma, lots of boys."

"I wore black slacks, T-shirt and cashmere sweater, with patent-leather shoes. It was just going to have to do. My father had hired an entire staff of caterers; I was surprised. They served cucumber slices with cream cheese and caviar, pea pods split and stuffed with cream cheese, a smoked turkey, and a whole poached salmon, like the kind you get at a good buffet. Mel and Peppie came early. Mel, with his ever-present unlit cigar, wisecracking, orders a martini. The bartender, who we talked to before the party got going, a guy in his thirties who was getting his doctorate in English lit, suddenly dropped the drink he was making and fell to the floor in a full-on grand mal seizure. Here's my dad holding him down, telling him he's going to be all right, and Bonnie goes and calls 911. Earlier that day, he had the first seizure of his entire life, and now he's having another. My grandmother says to me, "Wouldn't you know it, honey, that he'd pick a big party to have this happen?" I had to sit down. "Grandma, I don't think people exactly choose the time and place to get sick." I was nauseated and shaking and couldn't eat.

The paramedics came and took him away. As they helped him onto the stretcher, I waved goodbye to him and said, "Don't worry, honey. You'll be fine." But I wasn't sure about that. All his co-workers kept on serving. It felt as barren as the desert itself. I wondered all night if he was all right—and if anyone had come to be with him. He'd seemed so alone.

"I've been hangin' out with the Rainbow People, havin' a big festival, just livin' off the land, everyone pitchin' in and cookin' really good food, helpin' out with the babies, sleepin' in tents, tryin' not to be all sexual. It's real high, and I just came back to go look in on Daddy and Aunt Sister. Daddy broke his hip and I helped him around, wash some clothes, and then I'm takin' Jenny back out there, take her out of school for a few more days, it won't hurt her. Boy, when I heard you were comin' in, it was like a miracle, a celebration, and I just can't believe I'm sittin' here with you and you can finally see my baby. Jenny honey, don't be shy, sweetheart—go on, give Sandra a hug. She knows you. I don't know why she's bein' so silly. Are you tryin' to be funny, sweetheart, for Sandra? You remember her from the movie. She wants to be a movie star too."

There are memories that if left untouched will remain forever painfully romantic and unchanged. If you challenge them and go looking for them as they were then, they soon crumble, and nothing remains except the regret for digging too deeply into the privacy of your own recollections.

We sat on the edge of my bed in the Gainesville Hilton. I hadn't seen her in twelve years. I called her every New Year's, but now I was sitting right there with her and I didn't know how to talk to her anymore. I'd never thought anyone could be as beautiful and I never again thought anyone was that beautiful, but time takes its toll and I found myself walking nervously around my room, looking for a way out.

She was a stewardess for National Airlines when I met her, based in Miami, with a silver-streaked shag haircut and a smile so brilliant that it knocked me over in the orange groves of the kibbutz in Israel where I went to grow up and fall in love.

There were people from all over the world who volunteered to work on the various kibbutzim around Israel, and most of them were not Jewish. There was Clair,* a girl from Ireland, who sat around morose and beautiful, discussing her "bisexuality"; skinny white kids from England, who had never seen an orange tree in their lives; South Africans wearing bandannas and growing beards; an Australian on the lam from a bad life and taken up with a neurotic kibbutznik with three kids. I had roommates from Detroit and Brooklyn, Deb and Emily, who smoked; we would stay up all night, talking about life and guys and who was doing who.

When I drifted off to sleep at night, I was enveloped by thoughts of Fran* and her steel-gray eyes, which pierced through the darkness, her southern accent and funky kibbutz outfits left from the forties, and the feeling of acceptance by an older woman that I searched for, that haunted me and drove me to laying everything on the line about my most secret emotions.

We would run through the kibbutz at night, carrying a kerosene heater with rain sputtering off the top. Back to my room all cozy in flannel pajamas, smelling like Israeli baby powder and reading poems by candlelight and laughing at insane things she would say, like "Sandra, I'm all lathered up" or "Sandra, I got the squirty dukes." She was in love with a young boy named Bobby,* who was blissed out and a faithful follower of the guru Maraha Ji. I was always jealous and moped around, waiting for her to come by my room. They had a lot of sex in the afternoon and baked cakes. She was searching for deeper meaning to life and eventually went back to Miami to quit the airlines. When she was gone, I would listen to "Angie" by the Stones over and over and write her letters.

Once I came home I would hear from her sometimes, usually from a commune somewhere in Tennessee, always talking about getting back to the land.

Sally was sitting on the couch in the den, studying her face in a hand mirror, when I walked in. Without looking up, she asked me, "Do you ever just look at your face up close sometimes?"

"What for?" I said.

"You can learn a lot about your face."

"Yeah, like how many annoying things I see that I can't do anything about."

"No, things you can make better."

"Look, once I do my hair and makeup, that's it for the night. I never look in the mirror again until I get home and wash my face. The image of myself I leave the house with is the one I want in my mind for the evening; that way I feel confident and secure. What if my mascara ran or I don't have enough blush? It would just make me self-conscious, so staring in the mirror isn't going to make me feel any better."

"Well, I think it's good to look at yourself."

"I can tell."

I have many recurring dreams; they could be called night-mares, depending on how you view them. I dream about Madonna more than anyone I know (or don't know); some-how she's indelibly written into my subconscious, and the theme is always the same.

She's always very sweet and caring but unavailable. In one dream, I'm at my house in Scottsdale, Arizona, where I went to high school, and all the streets in my desert neighborhood are packed with tourists, as if there was some kind of a bazaar going on. Madonna is there, walking toward me, flanked by two bodyguards, right next to my elementary school, Cocopah. She needs protection so people won't bother her, but I want to be alone with her and become friends, so we start walking around the streets arm in arm, being very cool in black leather jackets, and I'm really trying to impress her and convince her that I'm wor-thy of her friendship. Then she has to get ready for a dress rehearsal of her show that she's doing in my backyard by the swimming pool. There's a lot of excitement, her show isn't really that great, it needs work and I want to help save her, but I'm having mixed emotions about how to tell her. She's running around in her black-and-red bustier, too preoccupied to notice me.

pamela tiffin—head of the national crisis center
fran lebowitz—secretary of the u.n.
jill st. john—assistant to the secretary of health,
    education and welfare
lesley ann warren—ambassador to the spiritual world
joey heatherton—special liaison between vegas and the
    white house
telly savalas—president
raquel welch—secretary of fun, fun, fun!

some of the nominees for my celebrity government.

The last man I trusted was Walter Cronkite.
    It's come to the point that I'm afraid to even fanta-
size about sex. I'll be lying in bed, dreaming about some
guy making love to me, and just as it starts to feel really
good, I'll make myself stop and think of something else.
It's just too fucking scary, even in my mind.

126

It's right about now that I could get into being promiscuous.

Just my luck that now that I'm ready to explore my sexuality, I'm forced into complete celibacy.

There is no fog here, I think to myself. Nothing mysterious or particularly intriguing. I keep driving despite my boredom. Can't anything unexpected ever happen here?

A kind of apathy settles in. I long for some emotion, anger, fear, happiness—any tiny bit of feeling. But nothing seems to come up.

I play with my radio. I've heard these songs a thousand times. I drive this street with my eyes closed. Suddenly I am awakened by a noise that terrifies me, humbles and excites me, all at the same time.

They are everywhere: in familiar cities, in little towns that sleep with an old-fashioned security. In rich suburbs they punctuate a tragedy; in foreign countries, sirens recall other times with sadness and nostalgia. They link the recent past with the distant future.

They are red and yellow converted Cadillacs and Chevy vans. They have drivers who have long forgotten fear, who have OD's on adrenaline, who never wash their faces or sit in the sun. They accompany the grim remnants of car wrecks—hysterical parents clinging to lost babies;

old women riding heavenward, quickly reviewing their facing lives. They are emergency vehicles, and these are the secret thrills they provide us with.

When I pass an intersection in Los Angeles and see flashing lights, the first thing I want to do is slow down to see if anyone was hurt. Not that I'm a great humanitarian, or that I've studied CPR and can keep someone alive until the ambulance arrives. There, I said it: ambulance. I wanted to save it for a minute. I wanted it to mean something when I said it, and it did, for me, anyway. It gave me a chill that no other word can provide.

I want to see what's going on. Is someone really hurt? Will someone be lying there, next to a disfigured, warped motorcycle, barely clinging to life, bleeding, praying, lost in another world? Or is someone just scraped, perhaps slightly bruised—a new ache, a trivial limp?

I want to see things that I would never want to have happen to anyone I love. They remind me just how precious life is; how it dangles; how threatened it always is.

When I was growing up in Flint, Michigan, a neighbor, the wife of a very successful man and the mother of three pretty little girls, had these middle-of-the-night nervous breakdowns. And I can remember hearing sirens —they woke me up in a neighborhood where nothing strange ever happened. They came and took her away and I wanted to know why. My dad would go out in his silk boxer shorts to see what was happening. (He did the same thing in a tornado.)

To this day I can recall the excitement of knowing that in an all-American family, someone was losing their grip. The thought of the family hovering together, crying, confused, lost, made me feel less old, and it also turned me on. It was as if I could go over and make everything all right. I could soothe the daughters, consult with the husband, reassure everyone that they could depend on me to take care of everything.

Sometimes in Flint, when the streets were iced over, two ambulances would collide. They'd have to send two or three more, depending on whether the drivers got hurt as well.

If I had the time, I would spend my days following ambulances to their destinations and riding to the hospital with the victims. I would hold them and stroke their faces. If they were unconscious, I would talk to them through the haze, telling them sweet stories. If they were conscious, I would comfort them and listen to what they were going through. If they wanted me to, I would kiss them. However, I would only kiss them if they were young and very good-looking. Well, they could be older, but they would have to be in great shape—at least before whatever just happened to them happened.

Whenever an ambulance races past me, I want to know who's inside. When they used Cadillac station wagons, you could see inside, and in winter it would make for a memorable sight as an old person was taken back home wrapped in a red blanket, a forlorn daughter sitting in the front, trying to decide what to make for dinner. The daughter is thinking: Well, I'm really glad she's alive and coming home, but this means I have to cook special meals for her, and I'm already exhausted. . . . God, I hate looking at overcooked vegetables, and of course, she's going to need help eating." It was a panorama—a painting Norman Rockwell forgot to paint: "Someone's Mother Home Again," in oils.

I hate the new ambulances because the windows are covered with reflective material and you can't see in. They're not as thrilling as the old ones. You can't share in the excitement. They're too private. Let's face it, an emergency is not some secret little moment, especially when it happens on a city street, or a department store, or a cafeteria. It's our right to see the results. If we saw the person collapse, then we deserve to know the outcome.

Sometimes, on an interstate, I'll see an ambulance pass by on the other side, lights flashing, not really driving that fast. I wonder if it's carrying a sick animal into town: a cow who can't seem to deliver her calf, a horse with a broken leg, a prize hog with a knife wound. I always think that out there in the open prairie, the rolling green hills where people just live and die, there can't be any real emergencies. A city is the only place that there are real emergencies, because it is impossible to drive fast to a hospital.

I guess that deep down we all hope for a crisis to happen right next door, so we can be gripped by something exciting and unexpected, like when the *Hindenburg* blew up —the ultimate spectacle. That is what emergencies provide. They are better than watching *Dynasty;* more thrilling than a Prince concert; more delectable than the best caviar. Someone hanging on to life is our best entertainment value.

Although we are all ashamed of ourselves for this, we have to admit that emergencies turn us on.

They're just a moment in time, at some strange intersection. They're nothing we have to commit ourselves to, or think about later, if we don't want to. But in that brief moment in which they occur, they take us away, as do the sound of a gun, the pierce of a knife, the dance on a thirtieth-story ledge, a heart losing its beat.

We can forget who we are. Our trivial problems take on less meaning. We are at once captivated and made human. We are the voyeur and the exhibitionist. We are forced to look at our own mortality for just about as long as we can without flipping out.

It is a secret thrill and a personal revelation as the ambulance pulls away with mock urgency and self-contained survival. You get to know someone new without ever asking his name.

I want to be on a plane this Christmas Eve, a long, long flight that lands in a strange midwestern town, where I don't know anybody. I can walk along deserted streets, past houses brightly lit and warm, all that familiar music seeping out under big, heavy doors.

I check into some small motel, where the maids

share cartons of Sealtest eggnog and whisper in the hallway early in the morning. I try to figure out what they're saying, but I turn over, falling back asleep. I dream about some Christmas a long time ago, walking to school in snowdrifts up to my chest. I keep wiping my nose on the back of my nylon glove; it gets all shiny and frozen. I keep falling over and getting up. The snow is flaking all over the world, it seems; big billows of steam pour out of passing station wagons. I'm just trying to make it home, for a big bowl of Campbell's bean-with-bacon soup and a bologna sandwich with Miracle Whip, cut crosswise the way our maid always does it, and just as I turn the corner onto my block I see an ambulance with its light turning, parked in my driveway.

All the neighbors are milling around, and no one can see me trying to run on the ice. I start to cry, and tears are stinging my chin. It seems to take forever, but I finally make it, and there's Fanny, our maid, on the stretcher, the whitest she could possibly be. My mom is holding her hand as they throw open the doors and carefully slide her in. "Don't pay this no mind, baby, it's gonna be just fine, now don't you go crying, 'cause I'll be back in a minute or two, come kiss Fanny now." I walk over and she tries to take off her oxygen mask, but the ambulance driver won't let her, and my mom is stroking her face. I lean over and kiss her on the cheek. "Merry Christmas, Fanny—I got your present. Can you wait just a minute and I'll get it for ya?" She never answers, and my mom tells me she'll be back as soon as she can. I go home to the neighbors', the Kaufmans, and try to eat their maid's tuna salad, but I can't stop thinking about Fanny.

When my mom comes to get me, way after dinner, she holds me for a long time and doesn't say too much. Back home, I hear a conversation between her and my dad as I mold Play-doh in the basement. I reach up and touch Fanny's Christmas present, a collage of bright tissue paper with a poem written on it.

I keep it for years and years and think of Fanny whenever I can't get home for Christmas.